THANK GOD AT ROCK BOTTOM, JESUS WAS THE ROCK THAT I HIT!

TRE LAVIN

authorHOUSE

AuthorHouse™
1663 Liberty Drive
Bloomington, IN 47403
www.authorhouse.com
Phone: 1 (800) 839-8640

© 2020 Tre LaVin. All rights reserved.

This book is a work of non-fiction. Unless otherwise noted, the author and the publisher make no explicit guarantees as to the accuracy of the information contained in this book and in some cases, names of people and places have been altered to protect their privacy.

No part of this book may be reproduced, stored in a retrieval system, or transmitted by any means without the written permission of the author.

Published by AuthorHouse 04/30/2020

ISBN: 978-1-7283-6072-0 (sc)
ISBN: 978-1-7283-6071-3 (hc)
ISBN: 978-1-7283-6070-6 (e)

Library of Congress Control Number: 2020907936

Print information available on the last page.

Any people depicted in stock imagery provided by Getty Images are models, and such images are being used for illustrative purposes only. Certain stock imagery © Getty Images.

This book is printed on acid-free paper.

Because of the dynamic nature of the Internet, any web addresses or links contained in this book may have changed since publication and may no longer be valid. The views expressed in this work are solely those of the author and do not necessarily reflect the views of the publisher, and the publisher hereby disclaims any responsibility for them.

Scripture quotations marked NKJV are taken from the New King James Version. Copyright © 1982 by Thomas Nelson, Inc. Used by permission. All rights reserved.

Scripture quotations marked AMP are from The Amplified Bible, Old Testament copyright © 1965, 1987 by the Zondervan Corporation. The Amplified Bible, New Testament copyright © 1954, 1958, 1987 by The Lockman Foundation. Used by permission. All rights reserved.

Scripture quotations marked NIV are taken from the Holy Bible, New International Version®. NIV®. Copyright © 1973, 1978, 1984 by International Bible Society. Used by permission of Zondervan. All rights reserved. [Biblica]

Scripture quotations marked NLT are taken from the Holy Bible, New Living Translation, copyright © 1996, 2004, 2007. Used by permission of Tyndale House Publishers, Inc. Carol Stream, Illinois 60188. All rights reserved. Website

Scripture quotations marked MSG are taken from THE MESSAGE. Copyright © 1993, 1994, 1995, 1996, 2000, 2001, 2002, 2003 by Eugene H. Peterson. Used by permission of NavPress Publishing Group. Website.

Anyone who ever thought God couldn't use you in your brokenness, this book is for you...may you find the strength to seek Him out and the fortitude to thrive in your place of destiny!

Contents

Acknowledgements ix
Introduction xi
Foreword xiii

Chapter 1   Rock Bottom 1
Chapter 2   Getting Help 7
Chapter 3   Who Are You Now? 13
Chapter 4   Life and the Living Word 21
Chapter 5   (Legal) Fightin' Ain't Fair 28
Chapter 6   The Prophecy 39
Chapter 7   Standing Firm in Confirmation 49
Chapter 8   Family and Spinal Fusions 60
Chapter 9   Destiny Fulfilled 69
Chapter 10 Your Pulpit Is in the Field 77
Chapter 11 The Setback 86
Chapter 12 Not Their First Choice, Just God's 93
Chapter 13 Transitions and New Starts 99
Chapter 14 The Mind Struggle is Real 106
Chapter 15 Prospering in Purpose 114

About the Author 119

Acknowledgements

Dear God, only You truly know how close to the end I was amid my brokenness. Thank you for using my broken pieces to craft a picture of redemption that only You could write and redefining my purpose in You for Your Kingdom.

To my beautiful daughters (the two things that I did right in this life) thank you for loving me despite my destructive choices. I am truly thankful that you got the absolute best of me and your mother. I pray you will be able to look at me and see not only God's redemptive power but that anything is possible to him that believes (MARK 9:23)!

Big Brotha Boaz and Sista I know beyond a shadow of a doubt that I would not be here today if not for your phone call. The depth of our friendship and love runs deep. If I could return half of the love and support you have shown I would truly be doing something great! May you soar to greatness in your overflow season!

Big Brotha Light Man we are coming up on twenty years! You have been a witness to most of the triumphs, failures, and missteps in my adult life. Thank you for giving me the truth that always has kept me from straddling fences and giving me strength, especially in my darkest hours! You make the Word written in Proverbs 27:17 a reality because you truly have been there to sharpen iron! I love you!

Dr. P where do I even start? You forced me to touch the deepest parts of myself and confront my truth. Being here now is worth it especially through the times that you had me on the extreme side of mad. Many of the anecdotes you taught me are still being used today. Though I am no longer a client I am forever thankful that I was because I would have never been challenged to grow and prosper through the valley of my pain. Be blessed as you are a blessing!

Ms. Amber Rusk your no-nonsense structured approach was what I needed post incarceration. As my probation officer you have supported my desire to be the best that I could be. Without your valued advice certain things would have been much harder to accomplish. Thank you for your compassion and steady hand. I greatly appreciate the fact that I crossed paths with you. God Bless!

Momma Al I am grateful for you accepting me in the authenticity of my truth. It has been my privilege and honor to build a strong relationship with you. Thank you for trusting me with what is most precious to you. Love you Dear!

Tweety I am honored that God sent you to me! Just when I thought that I would not be able to love again and that I was not worthy of being loved He reshaped my destiny. I cannot wait for you to achieve greatness and I stand and applaud you now for the best of what God has yet to reveal. It's time that you won. May you open your heart to receive everything that God has for you! I love you always!

Introduction

What happens when the outcome you've been working toward ends up being the outcome you least expected? Even if you knew in the back of your mind it was inevitable you still hoped against hope that it would turn out differently? In my case I broke, totally...*completely*...yet, the thing that finally broke me was not one singular thing but rather an accumulation of things that just snowballed. It's like the snowball had been rolled uphill and then just like that...*BOOM*...a freefall, straight downhill with no brakes!

This is my story of release, recovery, and redemption. Walk with me as I explore what it means to find God in the darkest of places and witness the real struggle as I hold on to Him and ultimately find my way from the depths of the pit and learn to soar above unforgiving circumstances on the way to my destiny and purpose.

> **And He said to me, "My grace is sufficient for you, for My strength is made perfect in weakness." Therefore, most gladly I will rather boast in my infirmities, that the power of Christ may rest upon me.**
>
> **2 Corinthians 12:9**

Foreword

"Blessed be the God and Father of our Lord Jesus Christ, who has blessed us with every spiritual blessing in the heavenly places in Christ, just as He chose us in Him before the foundation of the world, that we should be holy and without blame before Him in love, having predestined us to adoption as sons by Jesus Christ to Himself, according to the good pleasure of His will, to the praise of the glory of His grace, by which He made us accepted in the Beloved." ~ Ephesians 1:3-6

This scripture reminds me of Tre LaVin; it centers on our Redemption in Christ. At some point or another, we all need redemption; that is to have another chance in life after a mess up (or even several). When I met Tre, he was already in the midst of a storm of life which had been brewing for a long while. I would frequently say to him, "I don't have any magic fairy dust to sprinkle on you nor do I have the power to change you; you'll have to do your own changing but I will walk with you through it." This declaration was meant to be reassuring and comforting because I really meant it.

As a consequence, I was privileged to be able to help Tre rediscover a part of himself that had been lost and/or over shadowed. I encouraged him to journal and write down his thoughts and feelings and then read it aloud so he could hear himself to better understand the depths of his soul. He listened and you are the beneficiary of that process which is in your hand.

So, as you read this autobiography, you will enter the eye

of the storm feeling every detail of the life of Tre LaVin, as he paints a vivid picture from the inside of brokenness and despair to come to the place of excitement, joy and the peace of God's understanding and redemption. Tre shares his journey in an effort to help others. He pays it forward in an easy reading format. There is a quality about the writing that will lead the reader to pose the thought, "If God can use him then just maybe He can use me too." This is a journey worth taking and an investment in yourself, if you are interested in finding out just how much God's love can help, heal, and restore. Don't miss it, read on...

~ Dr. P.

1

Rock Bottom

Thank God when I hit rock bottom, Jesus was the rock that I hit! Sunday December 17. I was restless in the overnight hours. I didn't sleep at all. In fact, I cried all night December 16th. My life as I knew it was over! My wife handed me divorce papers. I did not say much. She did most of the talking. Even though I knew this might be coming I was still in a frozen state of shock trying to process what she was saying.

I had been out of prison a mere four months at this point after serving 13 and a half months of an 18-month sentence and I was now a felon on 10 years of supervised release. The circumstances that surrounded my incarceration had broken the valued trust of my family. For 3 and half years previous and up to that point what I had done put my wife and two daughters through absolute hell. My wife just needed to be released from the nightmare. So, while I did not want this outcome it was what it was, and I had to respect her decision. It would take me a while to get to that point though.

At 5:45 am on this Sunday I got in the shower and tried to collect myself. I got dressed for church and sat down, still numb. I had every intention of taking my daughters to church, spending time with them after, and then returning to my apartment in Horne an hour and 40 minutes away. Now, everything that I had been dealing with to that point landed squarely on my back. There were no less than nine things weighing me down: a civil case that had been brought against me in Federal court, the broken state of my marriage, trying to rebuild the relationships with my daughters, PTSD (with anxiety and major depressive disorder), learning to function in my new felonious probationary status, chronic neck and shoulder pain, financial issues, a job search that was becoming fruitless, and lastly those divorce papers.

Just after 6:15 am I got in my car to take a drive. Whenever I needed to clear my head I would either go for a walk or a drive. Being that it was dark outside, overcast, and raining I chose to go for the drive. I headed for the gas station to fill up my car. Once I got there and as I was paying for the gas everything started going dark. My tear ducts were overflowing as I had yet to stop crying. My ears were ringing (I suffer from tinnitus), my neck and right shoulder were burning in a way I had not experienced to that point, and I was having a very serious anxiety and panic attack.

I began to wonder out loud, "Do I even matter?" I could not see the point of existing in a world without my family, unwanted. Nothing, at all, seemed to be going right. As a pastor I know full well the Scripture found in 2 Timothy 1:7, which reminds us: "For God has not given us a spirit of fear, but of power and of love and of a sound mind." The enemy had shattered my confidence, I was walking in weakness, and seemed to be internalizing hatred and rejection on every side. Right then I reached a place that I only had nightmares about previously. I seriously wanted to end my life. Before now I had never actually thought about a plan but that all changed in that moment.

I had a fresh new bottle of trazodone, the medication I take to help me sleep. Thirty pills. Somewhere in my mind I had convinced myself that I would pull my car over in some desolate place and take the pills 10 at a time over the course of thirty minutes and pray I did not wake up. But before I could do that, I had to say thank you and let the people dearest to me know that I loved them.

Just before 6:30 am I sent out two text messages. I do not remember everything that I sent my wife in the text that I sent but I remember telling her something to the effect of: "she may actually be better off if I were dead and that maybe the four other times that I actually contemplated suicide were actually meant to be something"…then I sent a text to other family and friends that read: "Thank you for all your love and support. I literally do not have the strength to fight against myself. I love you."

You must understand that I am not a negative person at all. I am forever the optimist, always looking at the glass half full and looking for the absolute best in everyone. I am always the one encouraging everybody else with texts, phone calls, and the like. So, for *me* to send a text like that was not normal and immediately everyone knew something was seriously wrong. As I was driving my vision blurred, my ears were still ringing, and I was shaking uncontrollably. As I would come to find out later 33 phone calls and 17 text messages would come to my phone in the next 45 minutes or so.

Initially I am not sure how many calls I missed before I heard God clearly say, "Tre answer the phone." At this point I am wailing out of control, but I listened to God in that moment. Through the tears I answered, "God bless, hello" as I usually do. On the other end of the phone were my friends Daniel and Grace. In that moment God started to break through.

Even as I write this, I can still visualize that exact moment when Daniel said, "Thank God you answered." He and his wife Grace did not have the words for me, so they just let God take over. But something Grace said in that moment froze me. She said, "Tre, I can't even image what you are going through but it can be okay. I am not here judging you, I'm here to listen… whatever you need we are here."

Over the next few minutes, I do not recall most of what was said but at some point, Grace said, "Tre are you driving?" I told her that I was. She and Daniel pleaded with me to pull over. Eventually I did pull over, completely unsure of where I was. When I looked around all I could see were patches of fog and grass. After a few more agonizing minutes I got off the phone with Daniel and Grace who prayed that I would be able to have God's power wash over and guide and that the Lord would be able to cradle and protect me. They told me they loved me, and the call was over.

I knew things were headed south in a hurry because I could not think of any good thing to make me want to go on at that point.

NOTHING! Somewhere along the way the enemy had clouded my judgement so much that I could not even see that my daughters, ages 14 and 7 at this point, were reason enough for me to keep living.

Still in a daze, I put my car in drive and started to pull off again. My head kept pounding and the anxiety attack ratcheted up to another level. There is really no comparison here but looking back I felt a lot like Job. If you remember Job lost a lot while enduring his trials: his status in the community, the wealth he accumulated, his children, and his health. I really felt like with all the things I had done wrong to that point I was being punished and I did not deserve to be here. In Job 7 Job felt like there was no point in his life. The Message translation of Job 7:1-6 details his struggle quite thoroughly:

"Human life is a struggle, isn't it?

It's a life sentence to hard labor. Like field hands longing for quitting time and working stiffs with nothing to hope for but payday,

I'm given a life that meanders and goes nowhere—months of aimlessness, nights of misery! I go to bed and think, 'How long till I can get up?' I toss and turn as the night drags on—and I'm fed up! I'm covered with maggots and scabs. My skin gets scaly and hard, then oozes with pus. My days come and go swifter than the click of knitting needles, and then the yarn runs out—an unfinished life!"

Wow talk about raw emotion! Reality bites hard sometimes and as I came to realize later it was biting the hell out of me! With my ears still ringing I was unable to hear the phone calls that were coming in. I am not sure how many minutes passed but a while had passed before I heard God say again, "Tre, answer the phone."

This time, my Veterans Affairs (VA) psychologist, Dr. P was on the phone. Previously I had gone through 18 months of therapy trying to right the ship in my life. Understand something, Dr. P ain't no joke. This woman brought an entirely different edge to the counseling process. She is a lover of Jesus, who happens to be a counselor, not the other way around. She empathized with me, sympathized, but ultimately forced me to touch the depths of not only my pain but also the pain I had caused so many others. I had been in counseling with her for so long that she could instantly tell where I was in my head. So, when she called, she knew I was in a bad place.

In counseling, Dr. P took me through the four steps of what would become my new normal. She made sure that I understood that there is no such thing as a do over, I just have to do better. Many times, I was stuck in the chasm between knowing and doing. Throughout my process I was constantly reminded that I could not make **permanent** decisions to fix **temporary** problems. I am telling you that without her phone call I would have made a **permanent** decision that no one that I cared about would be able to recover from.

When I answered her call, I was in a frantic state of panic. But she was extremely calm. She could tell by my breathing exactly where I was in my thought process. She had me concentrate on my breathing. Once I could speak, I told her the situation and she listened and asked me one question: "Tre, sweetheart, are you driving?" When I told her that I was, her response was simple, calm, and direct. She said, "Tre is that safe to do or would pulling over be better right now?" As she continued, she said a form of the one phrase that had been drilled into my head repeatedly, "Tre you **cannot** make a permanent decision to end your life... this too shall pass...this circumstance is only **temporary**."

I pulled over in a parking lot. I could not to this day tell you how I got there but I did. God bless Dr. P because she kept me talking and on the phone. Yet, even as she was doing that, I was opening that bottle of trazodone. I had made up my mind! I was about to ingest all these pills and kill myself. Even with Dr. P's reassurance I could not see a better way. There was just one problem: my hands were shaking uncontrollably, and I could not turn the bottle over into my hand. With Dr. P still on the phone I got a knock on my car door window that would change my direction.

My wife, as I would find out later had called the police because she did not know where I was. There were literally officers out looking for me. How exactly did they find me? By pinging my phone. The policeman knocked on my window. I rolled down the window and he said: "Tre, you have a lot of people who care about you and they are worried about you. Your wife let me know the situation. I know you were handed divorce papers last night. But she asked me to remind you that even if the two of you aren't going to be together you still have your girls and they need you. You are an excellent father." He paused. "But your girls will never know how good you are if you take your life. I am aware of your legal situation as well. I am not here to arrest you. I am here to help you. Please, please just come with me and let me get you some help. I know you are hurting, and I know this is hard, but it can get better if you will just take the first step and come with me."

The officer saw my open pill bottle which by now had spilled onto the floor. I had a decision to make and there were two things, rather, two people whose faces God let me see in that moment that helped me make that decision, my daughters. I may have been broken but broken was better than dead and I knew then that I could not be any good to anyone if they were planning my funeral. It is extremely important to know that when we are in the midst of sin there is always a way out. Look here at 1 Corinthians 10:13 (AMP):

"No temptation [regardless of its source] has overtaken or enticed you that is not common to human experience [nor is any temptation unusual or beyond human resistance]; but God is faithful [to His word—He is compassionate and trustworthy], and He will not let you be tempted beyond your ability [to resist], but along with the temptation He [has in the past and is now and] will [always] provide the way out as well, so that you will be able to endure it [without yielding, and will overcome temptation with joy]."

Even amid my pain I was not alone and if you are reading this and suffering through the worst of what life has given you are not alone either! It was time for me to get help, not for anybody or everybody else, but for me. So, even though I did not know what lay ahead I took that officer's hand and took the biggest leap of faith I have ever taken in my life. Frederick Douglass once said, "It is easier to build strong children than to repair broken men." I was about to find out just how true that statement was!

2

GETTING HELP

The police officer told me to wait while he talked to the EMT's. I must admit I was terrified at this point because I was not sure exactly where they were taking me. But I was reassured that everything would be okay. They took my vitals. My blood pressure was sky high. I informed them that I was a type 1 diabetic. They checked my blood sugar. That was somewhere in the high 300's. They asked what my pain level was. Man, if I could have said 12, I would have but 10 was the max so I went with that. While I could hear what they were saying and was able to respond I was still disoriented, so much so that I was unable to follow the EMT's fingers. I was strapped to the gurney and transferred to Crossing Point Medical Center.

It also important to note that I am a United States Army and Operation Iraqi Freedom war Veteran. With that said, I should have been transferred to the Veterans Affairs (VA) hospital in Horne but for whatever reason I was not sent there first. Just after 9 am I was formally admitted to Crossing Point Medical Center. Over the next two hours I would recount the events that led me here four separate times. Once my medical team figured out a course of action, they placed a call to the mental health team at the VA in Horne. But it was Sunday and they were unable to get someone to pick up the phone. After repeatedly getting no answer they placed a call to the VA Medical Center in Walsh. The interesting thing about Crossing Point is that it sits almost equal distance from Walsh and Horne; 92 miles from Walsh and 95 miles from Horne. The next call was to the VA in Walsh and the people there answered.

There was one major problem though. Being that I was on supervised release I could not leave my extended surrounding living area without the approval of my probation officer, Ms. Amber Rusk. I texted her and let her know the situation. She called to check on me and reminded me that my health was the most important and just to keep her informed.

When things calmed down a little bit, I texted my wife to let her know what was happening. No response. I am not sure how many texts I sent her over the next few hours, but they all went unanswered. I also kept my Ms. Rusk informed like she asked. Eventually I was told that I would be headed to the VA in Walsh to undergo a psychiatric evaluation and to start getting the help that I needed. I was told that I was admitted under the veil of "suicidal thoughts with suicidal ideations," which meant that I not only had thoughts of suicide but also a plan to carry out the act itself. All told I remained at Crossing Point Medical Center for 12 ½ hours. Finally, just before 10 pm a police escort arrived to transport me to Walsh.

Over the next hour and a half, I thought a lot about Psalm 121 which in the NIV reads like this:

> "I lift up my eyes to the mountains—
> where does my help come from?
> My help comes from the Lord,
> the Maker of heaven and earth.
> He will not let your foot slip—
> he who watches over you will not slumber;
> indeed, he who watches over Israel
> will neither slumber nor sleep.
> The Lord watches over you—
> The Lord is your shade at your right hand;
> the sun will not harm you by day,
> nor the moon by night.
> The Lord will keep you from all harm—
> he will watch over your life;

the Lord will watch over your coming and going
both now and forevermore."

I was truly by myself in this moment so the only one I could reach out to at that point was God. I was going to have to trust Him more now than ever, even if I was not quite sure what that would entail.

When you about to be admitted to a psychiatric ward they take EVERYTHING from you, phones, keys, literally everything. The main concern is trying to ensure that the patient does not have access to anything that could bring further harm to themselves. I was told to write down every phone number that I might need and to keep it with me. After my clothes and other belongings were secure, I was escorted onto the psych ward floor. I was officially checked in just after midnight on the morning of December 18th. A nurse came and sat down with me. They brought me some food. I tried eating while the nurse was talking but my appetite was nonexistent. For what seemed like the umpteenth time in the last 15 hours I had to recount the nightmare that I was stuck in.

The first thing that the nurse said to me was something to this day that I have never forgotten. She said, "Mr. LaVin I know you are scared but we are here to help you. Right now, you may feel broken, but God will make you whole. The question is are you willing to do the work to make that possible?" I thought about what she said for a moment. Through my tears I managed to utter a strong "yes."

As we sat the nurse let me know that there were people who would not be able to wrap their minds around what I was going through. She encouraged me to focus on me and getting better. She reminded me that if I did not get better nothing else was going to matter. I had to do this work for me. If people were meant to remain in my circle they would and if not, I would have to make peace with that at that time.

Something Colin Powell said rings true here, "None of us can change our yesterdays, but all of us can change our tomorrows!" But before I could even begin to think about changing a tomorrow, first I had to make it through the present day. Once I received my room assignment, I made my bed and laid down. As exhausted as

I was, I could not sleep so I laid there tossing, turning, and staring blankly at both the ceiling and the floor.

As hard as it was to admit at that time, I knew then that my marriage was truly over. Over the next three days I could not eat, and I was mired in the deepest depression that I had ever experienced. Christmas by now was five days away and there was no guarantee that I would be well enough to be discharged.

In the first few days on the ward I underwent multiple evaluations and tests. My medications had to be adjusted and as they were my appetite started to return. I found out that I was a good candidate for the 90-day inpatient program. If accepted I would be able to retrieve my things in Horne and upon return, I would have a room waiting for me. As I considered this option, I had to consider my job and my living status. I would have had to break my lease at my apartment and ask if my job could be held for me while I was away.

There were two other factors to consider here. First, the chronic neck and shoulder pain I was in was not getting any better. I had an MRI scheduled in Horne on December 27th that I could not miss. I already had one MRI on December 14th, but the results had yet to be revealed. Secondly, I was taking a narcotic as part of my medication regiment and one of the stipulations for acceptance into the inpatient treatment was you could not be under the influence of any narcotic.

The social worker that was assigned to me came with me to my interview to see if I would be accepted into the inpatient program. While I was waiting for that decision the results of the first MRI came back. I was told that I had a tear in the labrum in my right shoulder and chronic tendinosis in the actual joint itself.

Looking back, I can see that this is the point where God started to show Himself directly to me. Soon after hearing about the diagnosis of my shoulder I sat down to find a bible and start reading. I opened it to this passage found in Genesis 12:1 (NLT): "The Lord had said to Abram, "Leave your native country, your relatives, and your father's family, and *go to the land that I will show you*" (Emphasis mine). I did not quite know what that meant but in a matter of 30 chaotic minutes I was certainly about to find out.

Thank God At Rock Bottom, Jesus Was The Rock That I Hit!

As it turns out I was accepted into the inpatient program. I reasoned that this would be a good step for me to be in a secure environment. I did not *want* to stay in Walsh, but I knew I *needed* to go if this was going to have any chance of being successful. It was time to *do better*. There were no more *do overs!*

Upon learning of my acceptance, a call came over the PA system for my doctor to report to a conference room on my floor. Soon after, my nurses and social worker were called as well. Less than five minutes after they were called, I was called to meet them. A conference call had begun on my behalf. Because of the tear in my labrum, the narcotic that I was taking, and the pending MRI appointment in Horne my team thought it would be best if I returned to Horne to care for those issues. I let them know that I understood that and then they set in motion a strict plan and regiment that I was supposed to follow once I got back to Horne complete with face-to-face appointments with the mental health team and my primary care provider.

As glad as I was to be taking this step my anxiety was building for another reason. I got this news on Friday, December 22nd. Christmas was the following Monday and they told me that the absolute earliest I could be discharged was on Tuesday the 26th. Once again, I was left deflated. Even though I had the divorce papers my wife had said that I could spend Christmas with her and our daughters. Now that was gone and even worse, she no longer wanted **anything** to do with me. It was here that I realized that I could not be like the dog who goes back to his own vomit and repeats his folly like a fool (see Proverbs 26:11). This was God setting the way for me to go to the land that he would show me. That land was, indeed, Horne. Though I was already living there He was letting know that was where I needed to stay.

That weekend was one of the longest I have ever endured. Even though there were people around me I still felt like I was all alone. All I wanted to do was spend time with the people who mattered in my life. My social worker jolted me back to earth when she told me that I could no longer put my focus on them and what I could not control. It was time for me to be selfish in this recovery process and realize that ***I mattered***! I had to start handling my own affairs once and for all. That meant I had to separate myself from my wife financially and otherwise.

Christmas day came and went. I made it through, but I was literally in a trance for most of the day. I was disconnected from everything or at least it seemed that way to me. The following day I would be discharged but there was just one problem. I did not have a way to get back to Crossing Point. I placed a call to one of the men in my church, the leader of my Sunday School class, and he let me know that he could come and pick me up and drive me back to get my car.

The bus would take me from Walsh to Terry where I would meet my Sunday School class leader. It was good to see a familiar face. He had been a wonderful support for me before, during, and after my incarceration, as had the entire class. We had a great conversation on the way back. We made a stop at Dairy Queen and sat down to have a quick bite to eat.

We got to the bottom of some truths at that point and got on the same page about how they could help me moving forward as I got back on my feet. Once I told him all that had been going on with me, he agreed with the assessment of my social worker. It was indeed time for me to start handling my own affairs. He assured me that whatever support I needed would be there.

We got back to Crossing Point in the rain. I thanked him for driving me back. He prayed for me and waited for me to get into my car. Once I got in my car and prayed, I had a decision to make. The sky looked the exact same way that it had on the 17th of December. I put the car in drive and headed home. I had a flashback to those deep moments of despair, but I was determined to move forward. Even if moving forward meant that there were more questions than answers...

3

WHO ARE YOU NOW?

I made it home. But being there felt weird. This was the first time that I was forced to face the fact that I would not be returning **home** to the family that I had spent 15 ½ years of my life with. After spending so much time building a life with my wife and children I truly felt out of place. Not being able to call made it worse. But I had to answer an extremely difficult question, "Tre, who are you now?"

In order to begin to answer that question I had to rid myself of all expectations of how I thought things should go. I had to become an empty vessel. I leaned on 2 Timothy 2:20-21 for guidance: "But in a great house there are not only vessels of gold and silver, but also of wood and clay, some for honor and some for dishonor. Therefore, if anyone cleanses himself from the latter, he will be a vessel for honor, sanctified and useful for the Master, prepared for every good work."

I had made more than enough bad choices and destructive decisions to this point and I truly knew the price of being willfully disobedient. *Full disclosure: the price is steep! That disobedience cost me everything, including my good name!* If you are stuck wondering if it is worth it to do things your way instead of God's way: **IT'S NOT!** The shrapnel left on that path leaves scars that could take an entire lifetime to heal from if you are fortunate to heal at all.

The first thing I had to do was open my own separate bank

account, but I did not have the money. I placed a call to Daniel, and I let him know the situation. He simply asked me to let him know how much it would cost to open an account at the credit union where I was. Part of me was ashamed that I did not have the $55 necessary to open the accounts myself.

Daniel put a stop to my pity party immediately. He said, "Tre you have been a blessing to so many others for so long, it's time for us to bless you, so please just let me do that for you now. Give me a minute and that money will be there for you. It's time for you to take care of you." So, once the money arrived, I opened an account at the Credit Union inside of the Horne VA.

Something important to note here is that in September of 2018 I had been hired on a conditional basis as a Food Service Worker in the Nutrition and Food Services department at the Horne VA, pending clearance of a background check. I never had a problem clearing a background check before my time of incarceration but by now it had been three months and I still had not been formally hired, which means I had yet to start. More on that a little later…

In the meantime, I was working as a dishwasher at a restaurant in downtown Horne making $8.50 an hour. With my new situation that was not enough money to even scrape together so I had to negotiate to see if I could get a raise. I presented my case and let my boss know about the cooking and food service background that I had and asked if he would consider allowing me to be a grill cook as well so I could make ends meet. My boss agreed and I got a raise to $9.50 for my dishwashing duties and I was going to be a grill cook on the Saturday morning shifts at $11 an hour. Being able to do that allowed me to make an additional $148 a pay period.

God was really covering me because the church I had attended in Crossing Point was paying my $710 a month rent, affording me an opportunity to save what little I could. That bit of obedient generosity saved me. Meanwhile, I was welcomed back at work in a way that I did not expect. My co-workers, many of whom, had been incarcerated before, offered a bit of hope and solace from their own struggles that reminded me of what I had been told back in Walsh on the psych ward: ***I mattered,*** and I would be okay.

I went to my MRI appointment on the day it was scheduled. I had to be there at 5:30 am. As I showed up it was windy and cold which made my body extremely rigid. This MRI would focus entirely on my neck. As the technician was setting up the machine, I prayed that this would finally help me get a full answer to this pain that I had been dealing with for so long. The way that I was being positioned left me in excruciating pain, but I had to deal with it for the technician to get a clear picture of what he needed to see. It took some time but when the scans were complete, I felt better knowing that the answer to what had been ailing me was finally coming. Even as I was waiting for those results, I still had other important business to tend to.

My first mental health appointment back in Horne was with Dr. Bower, a well-respected psychiatrist in the VA system, on Thursday, January 4. I did not really know what to expect as I had only had Dr. P., a psychologist, in treatment before. I was anxious the day of the appointment because this was yet another person that I had to tell the gory details of what was, to that point, the absolute worst day of my life.

But I promised myself that I would take this step and I could not back out now. In the words of Dr. P, it was time to "fly or fall." Dr. Bower was an extremely calming influence. He let me know that he had read up on my file and that he would guide me toward as much help as I wanted to get. He would help me in this recovery process, but he was not going to force me to do anything I did not want to do. He said we would work *together* and that I was not alone.

Dr. Bower listened intently, and I could tell that he was able to sympathize with me. He did not give me advice as much as gave me helpful options which allowed me to make choices for myself, void of anyone else's expectations. After finishing my 30-minute appointment, he set up my next appointment but this time it was with his nurse. He mentioned that she may be able to help me understand things in a deeper context given my background as a pastor. I did not know it yet, but that appointment would really begin to shape my purpose in what was to be the next season of my life.

Very soon after my appointment with Dr. Bower the MRI results on my neck came back. I found out that I had a pinched nerve that was causing weakness in my right arm, hand, and fingers. I also had a bulging disk in my C3-C4 vertebrae, and a narrowing of my spinal column. These things coupled with the labrum tear in my shoulder and the tendinosis of the joint itself put missing pieces to my puzzle in place. Surgery was a possibility, but they wanted me to go to occupational therapy first.

My appointment with Dr. Bower's nurse, who I will call Diana, was set for Thursday, February 1st. For whatever reason I was not near as anxious for this appointment. When I walked in the Diana introduced herself and told me to take a seat. Her approach was completely refreshing as in talking to her did not feel like I was in an extra sanitized clinical environment.

The thing that really made the atmosphere different was the fact that it really felt like I was sitting down talking to one of my sisters or aunts, almost like sitting out on the porch on a sunny weekend day. She got the vital information she needed from me and then simply asked me to tell her what I had been dealing with. After a while she asked me, "Tre, what did you do to cause this breakdown?" I answered in the most honest and authentic way I knew how, having just read Ezekiel 36:25-26 (NLT) before I walked in, which reads: "Then I will sprinkle clean water on you, and you will be clean. Your filth will be washed away, and you will no longer worship idols. And I will give you a new heart, and I will put a new spirit in you. I will take out your stony, stubborn heart and give you a tender, responsive heart."

Knowing that I needed God to respond in a way that could move my mountain I simply told her how trying things my way had not worked to this point and that I was really beginning to see the difference between the worldly repentance I had known until very recently and the godly repentance that I now knew. My heart was different now and I knew it, but I still needed to walk out the faith steps.

In 2 Corinthians 7:8-10 (AMP) Paul explains the difference between godly and worldly sorrow this way saying,

> "For even though I did grieve you with my letter, I do not regret it [now]; though I did regret it —for I see that the letter hurt you, though only for a little while—yet I am glad now, not because you were hurt *and* made sorry, but because your sorrow led to repentance [and you turned back to God]; for you felt a grief such as God meant you to feel, so that you might not suffer loss in anything on our account. For [godly] sorrow that is in accord with *the will of* God produces a repentance without regret, *leading* to salvation; but worldly sorrow [the hopeless sorrow of those who do not believe] produces death."

Prison helped bring an entirely different perspective to not only how I viewed things but especially how I dealt with them. Until then, being completely honest, most of the times I had been deeply wrong I was only sorry that I had gotten caught. Being sorry that you got caught is the perfect example of worldly repentance. It produces bad fruit and death. Often, I knew when I needed to apologize but it had gotten to a point where I became a *professional apologizer*. The only problem with that is when you have to say sorry too many times, those you care about become completely numb to the action and thus lose trust and belief in the original intent.

In having to deal with myself the one thing that I came to see was that I could no longer blame other people for my own misgivings. As I began to take responsibility for myself and my past actions, I was disgusted with what I saw in the mirror. Finally, the excuses and lies I told myself got to be too much and I cried out to God and made the firm and concrete decision to turn away from my destructive ways and come back to God wholeheartedly.

It was time for me to not only walk with God but to continue to exhibit the behavior that was consistent with my new mindset. Acts 26:20 (AMP) lays out what I mean, saying, "but I openly proclaimed first to those at Damascus, then at Jerusalem and throughout the region of Judea, and *even* to the Gentiles, that they should repent [change their inner self—their old way of thinking] and turn to God, doing deeds *and* living lives which are consistent with repentance."

The time for talking was over. Now it was time to have my yes be yes and my no be no (see James 5:12) with no regrets! No longer could I make empty fruitless deals with God to try to manipulate my circumstance. I had to own *me*! I had to learn how to trust who God had placed in my life and begin to understand that this new puzzle that was being put together was one that I did not have the pieces for. I was running a completely different type of race now and I was no longer in control.

Look at what the Word says in Hebrews 12:1-3 (MSG):

> "Do you see what this means—all these pioneers who blazed the way, all these veterans cheering us on? It means we'd better get on with it. Strip down, start running—and never quit! No extra spiritual fat, no parasitic sins. Keep your eyes on *Jesus*, who both began and finished this race we're in. Study how he did it. Because he never lost sight of where he was headed—that exhilarating finish in and with God—he could put up with anything along the way: Cross, shame, whatever. And now he's *there*, in the place of honor, right alongside God. When you find yourselves flagging in your faith, go over that story again, item by item, that long litany of hostility he plowed through. *That* will shoot adrenaline into your souls!"

Jesus is truly the author and finisher of our faith. As this translation tells us He put up with everything along His way to His destiny's purpose. If I wanted to truly walk alongside Him as God's child, I had to prepare myself to do the same.

Getting back to my conversation with Diana and with these things in mind, I told her everything about how I got to this place and then God, again began lining things up. Diana asked me which part of Fowler Road I lived on (I stayed on the corner of Fowler Road and Briarwood Blvd.) Once I told her where I stayed, she said, "Something told me you lived right around there, do you have a church that you attend?" I told her that I did not but that I was looking for one. She reached into a basket and started pulling all these different CD's. Having now heard my story in full detail she started repeating, "Oh, this is a good one you need this one…" After about the 3rd time of doing this she began to tell me about her pastor, who I will call Apostle Jacob Henry. In all, I ended up with eight CD's that had different sermons on them.

"Dad," as she called Apostle Henry had made a huge difference in the lives of her, her husband, and their family. She told me her testimony and how the Apostle had really been present and a great source of support and inspiration in their great times of need.

As she was speaking with a great manner of conviction, a quote from Willie Jolley came time mind. Mr. Jolley said, "Inspire others! Do not try to impress them, but rather inspire them. If you inspire, you will not have to be concerned about the impression; it will take care of itself. Inspire people!" By the time she finished talking about this man I knew that I had to attend a church service and meet with him.

Diana told me that he would not be there on the Sunday coming up but that he would be there on Tuesday but if I was not doing anything I should come on Sunday. This appointment was supposed to last 30 minutes but with the way the Holy Spirit started moving I was there for three hours! I know what you might be thinking…*appointments should not last that long*, and you know you would be right. But when God is driving the bus, I have learned to just take my seat and ride. As it turns out all her appointments in front and behind me had canceled.

Moreover, she had called in that day to tell her boss that she would not be able to work that day because she was not feeling well. She called her husband to inform him and he told her that she needed to go ahead and go to work because she was supposed to help somebody that day. As it turns out, through God's divine appointment the somebody that she was supposed to help was me.

By the time the appointment ended we were cracking jokes and laughing like a brother and sister would. She even said as I walked out that she felt like she had gained a brother. Yet, the most impactful time during the session was when we came together to pray for one another. At times you can just feel the anointing in a room, and it was present that day! She gave me the church's address and told what time service started on Sunday.

Upon my leaving I was full of a hope that I had not experienced on this side of my recovery and I must say it felt great. I had something to look forward to and I truly could not wait. As a man of God even in this uncertain time I knew that it was important to ensure that I was in attendance in God's house. In order to really embrace the healing process, I knew that God could not be absent.

At this point I started to understand that the things that I had done were not a reflection of who I was. They were things that I did, and they were not a true reflection of my character. I did not have to let my past mistakes define me. I was at a crossroads and I had decided that I did not just want to exist, I wanted to stand up and receive God's best!

John Mason says, "Mediocrity is a place and it is bordered on the north by compromise, on the south by indecision, on the east by past thinking, and on the west by lack of vision." Understand that Proverbs 28:13 (NIV), speaks the truth saying, "Whoever conceals their sins does not prosper but the one who confesses and renounces them finds mercy."

My truth and my willingness to embrace it was about to set me free. I was looking for new life and I would not only find it in the living Word, but I would also experience it at The Word of Life Faith Center...

4

LIFE AND THE LIVING WORD

Remember I told you about that job that was on hold for me? Upon my return from Walsh in late December I called and emailed twice a week to check the status of the job. Each time I was assured that the offer was still on the table and that the background check had yet to come back. To this point they had not said no but there was not a yes either which made the time that had passed since September uneasy.

On February 1st I received a call from the human resources department at the Horne VA. The man on the other end of the phone introduced himself and immediately apologized to me. He said, "Tre I am so sorry that it has taken so long to give you a concrete answer regarding employment with us. It looks as though your paperwork was lost somewhere along the route after I turned it into my supervisor."

I was listening, taken off guard by his explanation but thankful that I was talking to someone who could give me some answers. As he continued, he said, "Listen, I am going to resubmit your paperwork today. You have my word that it is going to be processed this time because I am going to walk it through myself. Are you able to come in at sometime today? I just need one statement from you regarding your period of incarceration." Even as I was on my way to work, I turned around immediately and called my job and told them that I would be late.

When I arrived at the VA I went straight to human resources.

Tre LaVin

The man I spoke to on the phone came out to greet me and apologized once more. I went back with him to his cubicle and he pulled out a blank piece of paper. Before I could start writing he told me to come with him into the conference room because he did not want to put my business in the street and have people overhearing what was going on regarding my legal situation.

He said, "Tre I have already spoken to your probation officer and the references that you provided. You have been vetted and your character was something that they all spoke highly of. I assure you that when you write this statement and clear this background check you will never have to make mention of the legal situation again, not as long as you are employed with the VA."

I looked him in the eye and asked him if there was a catch. "Absolutely not! Your honest transparency is about to be rewarded. Chalk one up for the win column! Once this packet gets turned in your 'if' becomes a 'when.' We should have your answer in about three weeks." I wrote the statement that he needed, and I shook his hand and prepared to leave. But before I did, he looked me in the eye and said, "Brotha keep your head up, you've come this far, God's got you the rest of the way." I let those words sink in and then I headed to work. No one could take my joy that day. I really felt like I might win this time!

On Sunday February 4th I did indeed visit the Word of Life Faith Center were Apostle Jacob Henry is the pastor. Walking in was such a welcome feeling for me. I found a seat near the front of the church and as soon as I did Diana turned and waved at me with a big smile. I immediately felt at home.

I had not had a church experience like the one I had during that service in a long, long time. I felt a release that allowed me the freedom to just be who I was. I did not have to pretend in this environment, and I found security for the first time knowing all the battle scars that I had now endured, and I was not afraid to show them.

When the invitation to discipleship came, I could not contain my joy. A microphone was passed around for people to speak. Once I had the microphone in hand, I let the church know that I felt like I was home and if they would have me I would like to be

Thank God At Rock Bottom, Jesus Was The Rock That I Hit!

a part of the move of God that was happening with them and their congregation. They let me know that I would be a welcome and accepted member of their family.

After service ended, I was introduced to a few people and somewhere amid all the hugs I received I began to tear up. It had been awhile since I had been embraced in that way and I took the time to rest in that moment and I began to reflect on how far I had come.

When church ended, I was headed back to my apartment. Upon my arrival home I was going to eat some tuna fish and crackers for lunch. However, as I got to my car Diana and her husband asked if I would like to come and eat with them. I had not been invited out with anyone since moving into my apartment in September, a period of five plus months. For the first time in a while I felt wanted.

I followed them to Golden Corral. Once again, I was feeling ashamed because I did not have the money to pay for my meal. Diana's husband, who I'll call Chad, told me not to worry about the cost and just to try to enjoy myself. As we sat down to eat, I must say that it felt wonderful to have a time to laugh and have conversation with people that was not centered around my past or what I had done.

Chad and Diana share a deep love of music as do I. For the next hour Chad and I were playing a game of musical tag, in which one of us would play a song and the other must guess the song's title. We were each sure that the other could not touch our musical knowledge. On our trip back through time and musical genres I laughed in a way I had not done in years!

The game finally ended when we both ended up playing the same song at the *exact* same time. We both were laughing hysterically. At that point, Chad said, "I think we have a tie, no losers here," a sentiment that Diana agreed with. As I was getting ready to leave Chad and Diana asked if they would see me on Tuesday. They barely got the question out before I let out an excitedly firm "yes."

On my way home I was so excited. I could not wait for Tuesday to come. I felt like I had truly been excepted. If there were people like this at Word of Life, I had to meet the Shepherd of the house! I would get my chance on Tuesday.

When Tuesday came, I made sure to arrive at the church early. Chad and Diana saw me and asked how the last couple of days had been for me. As I was answering they let me know that they had already told Apostle Henry a little bit about me. With a glean in his eye, Chad asked, "Tre, you ready to meet Dad?" I said I was, and they led me to his office.

As I went in and introduced myself the Apostle extended his hand and gave me a hug. It blew me away how much we had in common. He had spent some time as the assistant principal at the same high school that my mother and aunts had all attended, Tilley Tech. In his professional life he had crossed many of the same paths that I did growing up.

I was intrigued by the knowledge he possessed and the journey he had taken to get to where he was now. He was down to earth. As I told him the cliff notes version of my story, which by this point, both Chad and Diana already knew, he challenged me with one simple question, "Tre, all things being what they are, son what are you going to do about it now?" That question would become a theme for me, especially moving forward.

The man caught me off guard when he called me "son." I felt a love deep in my spirit at that point that would come to sustain me for the journey ahead. He said as my spiritual father he would guide me forward. He reminded me of the story of Gideon in the bible and let me know that was who I reminded him of. He spoke of how Gideon did not think that he was going to be able to do what the Lord commanded, the doubt he had, and ultimately the trust he found to be able to overcome a great enemy. He told me that by standing up, owning my story, and moving forward I was a man of great courage! From that moment forward if he did not call me by my given name, he made sure to call me by my new *name*.

Gideon's story is told in Judges 6 and 7. In these chapters we come to see that Gideon is set apart to save the people of Israel from the Mideonites. The Lord had given the people of Israel to the people of Mideon because of the wrong that the Israelites had done in the sight of the Lord.

Gideon was harvesting wheat when an angel appeared and

let Gideon know that he was a man of great courage and that he was being called to save the people of Israel from the Mideonites. Almost immediately Gideon is filled with doubt, but he knows that the Lord is going to be with him for the task at hand.

Ten men, along with Gideon were purposed to take down the Altar of Baal. This enraged the people so much that they asked for the person who destroyed the altar to be killed. Gideon's father Joash tells the townspeople that he will kill Gideon himself to save his son if Baal is really revealed to be a god. Gideon needed some form of reassurance that the Lord was with him. So, he asked tested the Lord using a fleece. Look here at Judges 6:36-40:

> So Gideon said to God, "If You will save Israel by my hand as You have said—look, I shall put a fleece of wool on the threshing floor; if there is dew on the fleece only, and *it is* dry on all the ground, then I shall know that You will save Israel by my hand, as You have said." And it was so. When he rose early the next morning and squeezed the fleece together, he wrung the dew out of the fleece, a bowlful of water. Then Gideon said to God, "Do not be angry with me, but let me speak just once more: Let me test, I pray, just once more with the fleece; let it now be dry only on the fleece, but on all the ground let there be dew." And God did so that night. It was dry on the fleece only, but there was dew on all the ground."

Here we literally see Gideon doubting the Lord despite what had been done right in his face, not once but twice! But that was not all. The Lord then told Gideon to reduce his army to 300 men to take down 135,000 Mideonites. Gideon then hears from a dream of one of the Mideonites that his destiny is indeed to conquer Mideon. Ultimately, when the Mideonites heard the 300 trumpets of Gideon's army sound and saw the torches that surrounded them they turned on each other and fled. Talk about overcoming odds! Dad's point was that on the journey ahead I would encounter great odds but by trusting the Lord and doing as He said I was also going to be able to overcome them.

Dad knew of my ministerial journey and that I had attended Liberty University in Lynchburg, Virginia. It was there that I received an Associate of Arts in Religion, a Bachelor of Science in Religion, with a minor in Christian Counseling, and lastly, a Master of Arts in Pastoral Counseling. Apostle Henry let me know it would be his honor to have me as his "son." In turn, I let him know how privileged I would feel to call him my spiritual "Dad." Moving forward that would be the relationship that he and I would have.

Dad reminded me of all the people in the bible who overcame major obstacles to become great and do great things for the Kingdom of God. He said that if I was willing to serve, he would help me restore the place that I had forfeited in the Kingdom. My status as a pastor would not be in jeopardy, but rather it was time for me to help rescue others. He was struck by my humility and willingness to be open.

The purpose God had for me would be revealed in the days to come within the words found in Acts 26:16-18:

> "But rise and stand on your feet; for I have appeared to you for this purpose, to make you a minister and a witness both of the things which you have seen and of the things which I will yet reveal to you. I will deliver you from the *Jewish* people, as well as *from* the Gentiles, to whom I now send you, to open their eyes, *in order* to turn *them* from darkness to light, and *from* the power of Satan to God, that they may receive forgiveness of sins and an inheritance among those who are sanctified by faith in Me."

Dad asked, "Son, are you ready to win the fight of your life?" I told him that I was and then we went into bible study. As Dad began to teach, I reflected on the promise that he spoke over me and the way I felt when I walked into his presence. The anointing of God was truly present in that meeting and I knew in meeting

Dad that I was in a safe place and that I would be ready to prosper above the valley of my pain.

I was not looking for a pulpit. I was looking for a safe place where I could sit still, learn, and be challenged in the Word. I found exactly what I was searching for when I walked into the doors of the Word of Life Faith Center. But more than that I encountered a Word that was living and active (see Hebrews 4:12) and I found a true source of new life!

On February 26th the VA called me back. When I answered the phone, I heard these words, "Congratulations, Tre, your background check has cleared. Welcome to the VA family. You will have a start date of March 4th, with new employee orientation to begin on Monday, the 5th." I was so relieved. I had applied for that job way back in July of 2017, and by now I had waited *seven* long months to hear those words. During that time, I came to see that my God did supply all my needs (see Philippians 4:19).

Because of all I had endured to that point a deeper level of humility rested with me. Those lows helped me appreciate that place I got to on the journey back up. For the first time in three plus years I was going to have not only natural job security, but a spiritual support that would surround me, and people who would help me not only walk out my truth but also my true calling!

5

(Legal) Fightin' Ain't Fair

Over the next three months even as things were looking up the enemy was still hitting hard. I had tangible backup this time though. The people of Word of Life would step up and support and cover me in prayer during this time of uncertainty, especially the ministerial team.

The church had established a prayer line, Monday through Friday from 6 am to 7 am, that allowed us to call in with our prayer requests and start our day covered with the Word. This would be a solid spiritual foundation piece that helped me endure many of the trials I was still experiencing.

The first test during this period came with my pending start at the VA. They sent me an offer letter confirming my start date. Once I received it, I gave my two weeks' notice at the restaurant. Three days after I did though human resources called me and said that some of my paperwork was processed after some deadline and they would have to move my start date back a full two weeks to March 18th.

The people at the restaurant did not waste any time filling my position and redistributing my hours to other people so I would not be able to return there. But I still needed to earn a check because I would be going three weeks without one when I did start at the VA. From the looks of it I was going to have to wait even longer. Max Lucado gives a great explanation of what waiting is, saying, "To wait, biblically speaking, is not to assume the worst, worry, fret, have demands, or take control. Nor is waiting inactivity. Waiting is a sustained effort to stay focused on God through prayer and belief."

With that in mind, immediately I began to pray with a belief that He would answer, and God told me who to call. I called one of my former bosses who had since retired but we maintained a solid friendship in the years since. Much like Daniel had done previously she simply asked how much money I needed. At first, I did not know. She then told me to add up all my monthly living expenses and give her that total.

That total ended up being $735. I did not want a handout though. I told her to set it up as a loan and hold me accountable to it. She gave me 45 days past what the new start date would be. I assured her that it would be paid back before then.

I was so thankful that God had answered my prayer! He was coming through. When you are obedient to the tithing principle God will indeed show up and show out. There were times in my natural mind that I wondered how I would make it because after tithing and paying the bills that I had there were times where I had $25 left for the entire **pay period**! But I could not be selfish with what was God's. I was still determined NOT to do things my way! I tested God by His Word in Malachi 3:10-12 (NIV):

> "Bring the whole tithe into the storehouse, that there may be food in my house. Test me in this," says the Lord Almighty, "and see if I will not throw open the floodgates of heaven and pour out so much blessing that there will not be room enough to store it. I will prevent pests from devouring your crops, and the vines in your fields will not drop their fruit before it is ripe," says the Lord Almighty. "Then all the nations will call you blessed, for yours will be a delightful land," says the Lord Almighty."

Now I could see just how God was making a way for me *because* I honored Him first and foremost. Saturday, March 3rd through the early morning hours of Monday, the 5th was extremely anxious for me.

A lady from human resources had called on Saturday morning and let me know that she was going to do all she could to get me to start on the coming Monday. The credentialing system had gone down and slowed the process. She told me to stay by my phone in the coming days.

I went to church that Sunday and my fears relaxed a bit as I listened to Word and internalized the worship experience itself. I let the congregation know about my prayer need and I placed that need on the altar. I was reminded again how far I had come and that the Lord would continue to provide for me. At some point, a lady sitting behind me took note of my singing voice and asked if I would consider joining the praise team.

After service, I went to ask the praise team leader what the steps were for me to join. She told me that I would have to audition and attend three rehearsals before I could "touch the stage." I did not have a problem with this. As I stated earlier, I was looking to serve in keeping with Dad's challenge to me in our initial meeting. The praise team leader told me when rehearsals were and what time to be there. Being a part of this team would prove vital for me from a support standpoint, as I now had something else to look forward to.

Monday morning came with still no word from human resources. At 7:17 am I began to pray, "Dear God, I thank You for who You are not just what you can do. Thank You for renewing Your mercies for me this morning. You know my exact need in this hour. I pray that you clear all the clutter and the mess to make this situation clear with a concrete way forward. Provide for me now as I continue to trust You. By the authority of Jesus Christ and in His Mighty Name I pray, Amen!" I still had my clothes laid out as if I had somewhere to go. I sat down to eat breakfast and read the Word. As I opened it up, I came to Isaiah 58:9-12 (NIV):

> "Then you will call, and the LORD will answer; you will cry for help, and he will say: Here am I. "If you do away with the yoke of oppression, with the pointing finger and malicious talk, and if you spend yourselves in behalf of the hungry and satisfy the needs of the oppressed, then your

light will rise in the darkness, and your night will become like the noonday. The LORD will guide you always; he will satisfy your needs in a sun-scorched land and will strengthen your frame. You will be like a well-watered garden, like a spring whose waters never fail. Your people will rebuild the ancient ruins and will raise up the age-old foundations; you will be called Repairer of Broken Walls, Restorer of Streets with Dwellings."

I spent a few minutes studying this passage unable to shake the promise. I fell on my face and began to worship the Lord in pure thanksgiving for who He is.

During my worship at 8:06 am my phone rang. I started not to answer because I was spending time with God, but I went ahead and picked up. As I came to see not only had I answered but God **answered**! The lady from human resources was on the phone. She said, "Tre, how long will it take you to get to the VA, I was able to get everything completed and there is a spot for you in orientation today, can you get here?" Without realizing it the first thing I shouted was, "Hallelujah to the King of Kings!" Once I caught myself, I managed to answer her question, telling her I could be at the VA in 20 minutes. Her response: "Amen, glory to God! They have just started but whatever you miss we will catch you up. Congratulations we will see you soon."

As I hung up, I burst into tears! God did not forget about me. He had not left or forsaken me (see Deuteronomy 31:6, Hebrews 13:5). I got dressed and I called my friend Wesley and let him know about the move of God that had just taken place. He said, "Amen, you have done the work that led you to redemption, now it's time **to *go to work***!"

There are a few things to know about Wesley. He has known me nearly half of my life. I met him and my wife at Fort Chambers, Kentucky while in the Army. He served as the best man at our wedding and was a dear friend of our family. I consider him to be the brother I never had. By this point he had been a witness, whether directly or indirectly, to most of the major milestones, missteps, and hurdles in my adult life. Because of this, I can always trust that he will tell me the truth. We can "cut through" each other and reach a place that not too many can. Outside of God, when I am struggling to make sense of something and need a male perspective, I will call him.

It was during this call that he did what so many before now had done; he reminded me of my renewed purpose! He told me that I had spent so much time *striving* and it was time for me to start *thriving*. I used to think that those were the same thing but there really is a difference. Merriam-Webster defines the word strive like this: "to struggle in opposition," and the word thrive like this: "to grow vigorously: flourish; to gain in wealth or possessions: prosper)." Many things that the enemy had stolen from me I was about to regain. I was not exactly sure how, but time would tell.

I finished orientation on Wednesday, March 7th and was able to report to Nutrition and Food Services that afternoon. It felt good to be in this environment knowing I would have steady hours and a steady paycheck with benefits on this side of incarceration. Over the next couple of days, I would be introduced to most everyone in the department. Some of the guys seemed cool and others I was told to avoid for various reasons but for some reason there was one person that I had yet to meet.

All told there were four people with the last name LaVin in our department. I had already met two of the three others but had yet to meet the last one. The first time I saw her I remember thinking, "Wow, she is beautiful and carries herself with grace." Even upon seeing her from a distance it would still be a while before our paths would cross. Besides, I had not been working here a week yet and I had a full plate already trying to balance out some other things at the same time. With my first check I did pay that loan back, as promised.

By now, I had been in occupational therapy for my shoulder injury for two full months. I was progressing well, and things were looking up. But the pain itself was still lingering heavy. The pain was constant, and it kept me from being able to get any kind of decent rest at night. I would lay down and within an hour I would be up having to change positions and attempt to get comfortable so I could go back to sleep. Since the beginning of the year I think I slept more than four hours straight in a night twice. This pain was no joke!

The therapist kept encouraging me, reminding me that pain was part of the recovery. So, I did my best to embrace it, but nighttime was the worst for me because the pain did not let up!!! Once a week though I kept coming to my appointments and pushing through the pain. Any relief that I could get had to be better than this high level of suffering.

Even in physical discomfort I found comfort in the Spirit through a verse in Psalm 34:19 (AMP), which reminds: "Many hardships *and* perplexing circumstances confront the righteous, But the Lord rescues him from them all." During this time, I only went three places, church, work, and my apartment. I was hyper focused on the tasks at hand and would not be distracted from the prize.

Work had been going well and by now I had completed my three weeks of praise team rehearsal attendance. Our praise team leader had a song in mind for me to lead on the first Sunday in April, which happened to be Easter. The song was "Worth" by Anthony Brown and group therAPy. She and Apostle Henry thought it would be a perfect song to sing given its redemptive lyrics.

The song's lyrics spotlight Jesus and His sacrifice for us as individuals; His sacrifice on the cross making us free, and whole, while giving us an opportunity to tell all we know about Jesus's love for us. Jesus came to change our lives simply because He thought we were worth saving. Furthermore, the song speaks of how we have been cleaned up from the inside and are worth being kept.

This song is made extremely personal because it is sung from the first-person perspective. It is like a personal love letter to Jesus. As I practiced the song, I could not help but think about all God had brought me through and how much He loved me, so much so that He showed up to stop me from taking my own life.

The praise team always dressed in a different color theme for Sunday service. For Easter Sunday we were supposed to wear white. In the weeks leading up to the big day Dad asked me what size suit I wore. I let him know that I wore a 42 long. On the

Tuesday before Easter he pulled me into his office and said he had something for me. He told me to wait a second as he went into his closet. When he came out, he presented me with a beautiful cream-colored suit from the Steve Harvey Collection.

He said that he would be honored if I wore this suit on Sunday as it represented the new life that I was now living and that it would be the perfect way to stomp on the enemy's head and make a statement. I was overwhelmed as he told me to try it on. Once he saw how well it fit, he said it was mine to keep. I was calm in his office but when I got to the car, I needed a minute. The tears I cried were pure tears of thankful joy.

I woke up on Easter Sunday excited! The song I was leading was a perfect complement to my very own testimony. I wanted to represent God, Dad, and the praise team in a way that brought glory to God in the way that He deserved. It would be the last song before the sermon, so I had some time to center myself. I was nervous and that surprised me. I had been singing in church choirs and various praise teams since I was eight years old. But this time, this moment, felt different. As the song started, I belted out the lyrics strong but by the time it ended I had been overcome with emotion. God would not have it any other way.

The next fight that took center stage was visitation with my daughters. Because I wanted to take my own life my wife did not feel that our girls would be safe with me unsupervised. She was pushing for one hour supervised visitation in which someone would watch every interaction that I had with my girls. Inside I was a wreck because I did not know what all to expect.

I got some guidance from an unlikely source: Ms. Rusk. Knowing what I was up against and knowing that I could not afford a lawyer she gave me some information on the Father's Initiative which helped fathers fight to be a presence in their children's lives and provided a pathway to get legal representation in court cases.

I took her advice and contacted the American Family Law Center in Horne. They said that they could help me get my paperwork together for filing with the court but because my case was to be contested in Berk County and I lived in Hawkins County they would not be able to represent me in court. I would be responsible for the filing costs but those were separate from their original fee of representation. The total fee I was responsible for was $650 which they would let me pay on a payment plan.

My court date was set for Tuesday, May 8th. Before that day though Apostle Henry gave me a character reference letter. It spoke volumes about what he thought about me, especially knowing the full history of what I had been through. He did not speak of me like I was damaged goods.

Among other things, he spoke about my dedicated service to others saying, "His commitment to serve and be a blessing to others is to be well commended." He continued, "I have observed and watched Tre walk in sincere levels of truth...Tre is a catalyst of light and action. His desire to see others excited about their purpose and passion is a great gift inside of him."

Dad spoke highly of my purpose and path *forward*, not the other way around. Word of Life was not just talking about being a support, they were walking the action out. On one end I was armed with the spiritual support that I needed but on the other side I was missing the physical support of a *lawyer*, and as I would find out soon, it would cost me dearly!

As I sought out legal advice, one piece of it was constant, "Mr. LaVin, as a non-custodial parent you will not be able to get credit for paying child support if it is paid out of a joint account still shared with the custodial parent." Admittedly, I did not know how true this really was, but I was not a lawyer either. After a fifth lawyer reasoned the same thing, I started the process to have my VA entitlement moved into my new account and out of the account her and I shared. After all, I had already been in enough legal trouble and was still paying real consequences for that and I did not want anything to be the cause of sending me back to prison for any reason. Period.

I did not let my wife know that I was moving the money for two reasons: one, I was still going to keep paying the mortgage anyway until the court proceedings were over and two, we were not really speaking at this point anyway. So, I did not think the location of the money mattered all that much. I would be proven wrong, however.

When May 8th came, I drove up to the city of Benson where

our case was to be heard and waited for my wife and her lawyer to arrive. When it was our turn to appear in front of the judge, I gathered all my paperwork and began to pass out the relevant information to her legal counsel and the judge.

My wife's lawyer got to present first. He asked her a series of questions and then I had the opportunity to cross examine being that I was pro se and representing myself. I asked my wife why she was asking for so much money, especially given my current financial situation. She said, "Tre, *you* moved us to Crossing Point, and it costs a lot to maintain the cost of living." I did not have many other questions so soon it was my turn in the seat.

I told the judge that I did not believe it was fair that I had to pay so much money. My argument was that I still had to find a way to live and giving her so much would not accomplish that. What the judge said next flipped the entire course of the proceedings. She said, "Mr. LaVin, are you saying that you do not your children to have a roof over their heads?" My response: "No, ma'am, **but**..." That did it...if there was ever a statement I would have wished to take back; it would be that one.

The judge said this proceeding was not about me but about our girls. She said, "You will get time to address things pertinent to you but now is not that time." Of all the times to put my foot squarely in my mouth, I had picked the worst one! The discussion then turned to visitation.

The proposal called for one hour of supervised visitation. The judge granted me two hours. I did ask if there was a possibility to get more than two hours and the judge informed me that the center where we would conduct the visitations only offered two hours max. The earliest this could be changed would be when our oldest daughter turned eighteen, almost a full three years away.

In the state where we reside if a couple has been married for ten years, in a divorce one of the parties can ask for spousal support *in addition* to child support. The judge said this would be granted to my wife. All told, after factoring in child support, spousal support, and health insurance reimbursement my monthly amount due would be $1,956.11. It really is cheaper to keep her! The judge also ordered that the marital residence be put on the market for sale immediately.

Things had gotten so tense in the courtroom that morning that we were also ordered to get a membership with Our Family Wizard, a co-parenting app that helps parents in high level conflict situations find effective ways to work together for the safety and well-being of the children. In addition to the annually renewable membership, we, as parents, were ordered to take a course and submit the certificate of completion within 30 days. Instantly, my already heavy situation had gone from bad to worse. Just when I started to win, I lost...BIG!

The first supervised visit would take place the first weekend in June. When the day came, I had no idea what to expect. In order to keep things civil, the custodial and non-custodial parents arrive at staggered times so not to cross paths, with the non-custodial parents having to enter from the alley at the back door.

Once inside, I signed in and waited to be escorted to a room that was not really a room. Instead it was a hallway separated by three partitions that allowed four families to visit. We could bring lunch to eat with the children, but we were relegated to playing cards, board games, conversation, and absolutely NO phones, which meant NO pictures! Somebody would sit in a chair directly from across from us and take notes the entire time! While doing so, they would be watching and scrutinizing each move. Early on anyway, it was hard for anyone to be themselves.

The visit started awkwardly as the girls and I were trying to find our footing. It had been three plus months since I saw them last. We always had a great time centered around food so once we started eating that broke the ice. I asked them how they had been over the last couple of months. After about an hour we were able to settle down a little bit. When it was time to leave, I gave them a hug and tried to hold back tears. This was now our new normal.

I drove back to Horne in a funk. I laughed reflecting on the jokes we told and the laughs we had during the visit. I even put on some of our favorite songs. But I could not shake the enormity of what lay ahead. I would be seeing my children for a **total of 48**

hours a year moving forward with no time for any of the three of us to be ourselves, unfiltered.

In the shadow of my new normal it seemed like I had come to the end of the road in some respects. I still had a way around, but it would not be a simple route. There is plenty of truth found in this statement by John Capozzi when he states, "A turn, or bend in the road, is not the end of the road...unless you fail to make the turn."

6

THE PROPHECY

Even as I was going through this legal battle and headed for divorce officially all was not lost. Amid all of this I was beginning to find my footing at work. As I started to show reliability in what I could do I was receiving different taskings within the department. I was a tray passer, which meant that I was responsible for delivering meals to the bedside of our Veteran patients who had been admitted into the hospital and picking those trays back up after consumption. But on occasion I was asked to assist on the tray line when they were short staffed. Our tray line personnel were responsible for putting the food on the trays and setting the food transport carts up for service.

I am not sure of the exact day this occurred but at some point, I was formally introduced to that mystery woman with my same last name. I was told to "load" for her which meant I would be responsible for putting the completed tray inside the food cart and pushing the cart to the personnel that would set it in the docking station to be heated.

I looked forward to these opportunities because the tray line represented the next higher grade of pay and I wanted to learn all I could and become proficient so that I could be promoted and make more money with my new status and pending child support payments. Anytime I saw something new I was always asking questions to learn as much as I could.

By now I knew who everyone else in the department was,

so it was not hard to figure out the name of the last person who I had still yet to meet. As I approached, I said, "You must be Stella LaVin." "Yeah," she said. "Well, my name is Tre LaVin, I've been trying to figure out who all of us were who had the same last name. I was told that I would be loading for you today."

She would go on and give me instructions letting me know what I was supposed to do. She asked, "Are you kin to any LaVin's where I am from?" Having misheard her I initially answered "yes," but would correct myself when I heard her question clearly because I did not have any relatives where she was from.

One thing about the tray line: they always have music playing. It helps pass the time while working. This, of course, was right up my alley. Besides, this would help me focus on something other than legal battles, divorce, and the pain I stayed in.

As Stella and I began working side-by-side the music kept playing and I started to sing along. "You have a nice voice," she would say. After a while, as I kept singing these ol' school songs, she quipped, "Wait, how old are you? You are too young to know anything about these songs." Through laughter I said, "I'm 37." She said, "Wow, you look really good for your age?" "Thanks," I would manage. "But wait, how old are *you???*" "Me? I'm 40," she would say. As I looked at her all I could do was give her a high five and crack a smile. I was sure she was lying. This woman did NOT look one single day over the age of 32! You could not really hold a full conversation on the tray line but from what I could discern Stella was good people. Our vibe was a friendly one, nothing more it seemed.

Over a matter of a couple weeks I learned a little bit about her story, and I began to share my own. I did not have any friends this side of Horne outside of the associates I had at church, so it felt a little strange to be opening up to anyone because my story is not the easiest one to tell. But God told me this much, "Tre, you be completely authentic in your honesty and My truth and I will take care of the rest." In following His instruction, I was starting to gain a friend.

In gaining a new friend I had to remain faithful to the Lord and what I was being taught in this season because I had been released from bondage that I had created and was not trying to go back. I did not want to be like the unbelievers that Jesus was speaking to in John 8:31-36 (NLT):

> "Jesus said to the people who believed in him, "You are truly my disciples if you remain faithful to my teachings. And you will know the truth, and the truth will set you free." "But we are descendants of Abraham," they said. "We have never been slaves to anyone. What do you mean, 'You will be set free'?" Jesus replied, "I tell you the truth, everyone who sins is a slave of sin. A slave is not a permanent member of the family, but a son is part of the family forever. So, if the Son sets you free, you are truly free."

I now knew and understood just how much Jesus loved me and because of that I wanted to ensure that I did not lie to anyone about who I was BECAUSE of Him. In truth I had been freed. My legal situation was what it was, so I figured that if I told people my story and they decided not to have anything to do with me that was better for me. At least this way it would save me the trouble of getting too attached and being let down later.

Stella did not flinch. I talked openly about my coming divorce and my girls and what I was going through in the fight to see them more than I was. At one point, Stella said, "Wait, so you keep talking about your girls and the fight you are in, why are you even getting a divorce?" I looked her square in the eye and told her why. When I finished, she replied, "Well you have a good job, that's a start but God's got you so what are you going to do about it now?" This was now the second time that I had been asked the same question after telling my story, "What are you going to do about it now?

The question itself offered confirmation for me in that it solidified the steps that I had now been taking for a while. There was no time for me to look over my shoulder expecting my past to give something back to me. I had to keep moving forward and running the race set before me and I was determined, even more so now to stay in my lane and on track. I was seeking a prize that was not temporary. I wanted more! I had goals and I had to stay disciplined to achieve them. 1 Corinthians 9:24-27 (AMP) says this,

> Do you not know that in a race all the runners run [their very best to win], but only one receives the prize? Run [your race] in such a way that you may seize the prize *and* make it yours! Now every athlete who [goes into training and] competes in the games is disciplined *and* exercises self-control in all things. They do it to win a crown that withers, but we [do it to receive] an imperishable [crown that cannot wither]. Therefore, I do not run without a definite goal; I do not flail around like one beating the air [just shadow boxing]. But [like a boxer] I strictly discipline my body and make it my slave, so that, after I have preached [the gospel] to others, I myself will not somehow be disqualified [as unfit for service].

Stella gave me a window into her world. Blessed with five children, and herself divorced, she had been in a relationship for about four years. Out of respect for her and considering my own situation I never thought about crossing any lines to try to create something more than what it was.

She knew who the Lord was, and her boyfriend had been mentoring her in the Word. Still, there were things that she did not know, and she was eager to learn. She knew about my background as a pastor so many times she would seek spiritual guidance from me. As far as I was concerned, I was a friend who was called to help her along in her spiritual journey and I stayed firm in that.

In one fell swoop, however, our friendship could have ended before it ever really got started. Some co-workers had been digging around and some found out that I had been incarcerated. One day someone pulled Stella aside and showed her something. As they did, they told her, "Look at the kind of shit we got here working at the VA!"

I had not lied to Stella in the time that I had known her but hearing this news and reading whatever had been shown to her shook her. She could not believe what she had read, and she was feeling some type of way when she saw me that morning.

Up to now we would greet one another with a side hug. But this time was different. When I leaned in to hug her to pushed herself away. "Is something wrong," I said. She just looked at me flatly. "Hold on, what is going on?" I continued. She looked me dead in my face and said, "Did you rape someone?" I returned her dead eye look and said very clearly, "No, I DID NOT. Look at me. Seriously, LOOK at me, I do not have a reason to lie and I have not lied to you. Where did you get this from?" "I read something," she would say. "Well what you have read was what the prosecution alleged but that is not what happened and ultimately raping someone was not the reason I was incarcerated. If that was the reason, I would not be standing here talking to you, I would STILL be in prison."

She had believed what I told her leading up to this moment, but she had doubt after seeing what she read. After confronting me now, and from that moment forward, she did not doubt what I told her regarding my incarceration. I had owned my truth and I was going to continue to do so no matter what anyone said. Stella did not tell me who said this stuff to her, and it was a great thing that she did not because I would have lost my job that day.

Adversity had been a constant companion of mine for some years now, especially recently so I was not surprised at the attack. Yet, I was past pissed! But, in that moment, I had to catch myself. I could not fall apart now. I had already seen that movie. Cavett Robert says this, "If we study the lives of great men and women carefully and unemotionally, we find that, invariably, greatness was developed, tested, and revealed in the darker periods of their lives. One of the largest tributaries of the river of greatness is always the stream of adversity." Even though I cannot swim for real, in a figurative sense this was not the first time I had been swept up by the current of adversity and it would not be the last. As I would learn a little later, on the job front, I was just getting started.

Away from work I continued attending church but by now my

work schedule did not allow me to be off on Sundays, as we were on 4-week rotations. During this time, I would attend the midweek bible study and still attend praise team rehearsals even though I would not be there on Sundays to sing.

I was already ordained as a minister, a designation I achieved in 2012 upon my graduation from seminary school, so I was able to do some work with the ministerial team in some limited capacities. It was here that Dad first brought up the opportunity for me to formally be licensed to preach in the state. He laid out a plan and told me that I would have to attend some courses at the school the church ran, The Word of Life Bible Institute, of which he was the dean. I was looking to continue sharpening my spiritual sword and if this was a way to do that, I was all in. I was up to do anything that would keep my focus and I would attend the Saturday classes when my work schedule allowed.

Although Stella and I were work friends we had not exchanged numbers. As I continued to answer her random spiritual questions God started giving me more to tell her. One morning as we were talking God gave me more to tell her, but we did not have much time, so I asked for her number. She gave it to me but said, "Don't call a lot because he's (her baby's father) very jealous." I let her know that I respected that and that I would only call if God had something specific for me to tell her. Even so, over the course of the next few weeks I would only text a handful of times.

As I was in prayer early one morning God showed me Stella's face and how the enemy was working. The text I sent got her curious and started a different type of dialogue. Here is what I texted: "Stella, fix your face! It's time to wreck hell today! The lies being told about you are just fuel that is being used to ignite your breakthrough!" Her reply: "What u talking about? What lies?" I continued, "It's no one here at work but what I am seeing is that someone that you used to be close to is strongly trying to smear your name. You had previously given them the benefit of the doubt and paid dearly for it…but you are redeemed!" "Tell me more," she would say.

Stella was amazed at how I had heard from God, especially knowing that she had not told me anything about this individual or circumstance. Right around this time she began to recognize just how seriously I took my walk with God. As we were talking one day, I asked Stella, "Have you talked to God and asked Him for what you want." "Well yeah, He knows my heart..." I continued, "Be that as it may, Him knowing your heart is not enough. You actually have to be specific and detail what you want." "Really? I did not know that," she would say. By this point, I had been actively interceding on Stella's behalf for the relationship that she was in. A few days later I would text to say happy birthday to her son.

My birthday was coming up. In this new season I knew I had a lot to celebrate but I did not have anyone to celebrate with. One thing about a fall: as most people witness it, they will get out of the way and watch your world come completely apart and as you lay there broken, they will not remain to help pick up the pieces. I could talk to Stella, but I was not dare going to try to spend time with her outside of work. I respected that boundary too much.

Being in my apartment was a lonely existence. I did not have cable or a streaming service so I would watch movies on DVD and spend time in the Word. My phone was not ringing much, and I did not want to burden anyone, so I just stayed to myself. It did not help that I did not get invited anywhere either and the physical pain I continued to feel was chronic. In more than a few ways, I was in a hurt place. On Wednesday July 25th a day before I was to turn 38 something happened in church that would literally shift the course of my life yet again.

Payday was two days away and I had $15 to my name. My gas tank was on empty and I needed to eat as well that night. Just after 5:00 pm God spoke to me, saying "Tre, just make it to My house." Knowing that I heard Him, I was not about to be disobedient so I planned to go to church on the gas I had, and I would just catch the city bus to work for the next two days. I prayed and made my way to His house as instructed.

When I got to the church, I was excited because I knew God would not say what He said and leave me stuck out there, but I had no clue what he had in store. As I arrived one of the ministers came to me and as she gave me a hug she said, "Brother, God told me you needed this." She had given me $20. I said, "God is answering prayer, He told me to make sure I made it to His house tonight." She said, "God Bless you, glad to be obedient." The fact that God had provided for me in that way had me in a true state of worship. I thought that was the reason I was supposed to be there but there was more.

Apostle Henry prayed for me as bible study started and went on with the service. When he finished the sermon, he looked at me as I was struggling with the pain in my shoulder and said, "Come here, Son…" He said, "There is a Word from the Lord…" After pausing for a moment, he said this:

> "The devil is busy trying to pull the ministerial calling from your life and tormenting you daily… BUT…that call on your life has now been perfected. There is a wife being sent to you that will be able to come alongside you…she will embrace your call, understand your call, and not be threatened by your call. There will be a church for you and her to pastor."

Understand this. I was still going through a divorce and here God was telling me through Apostle Henry that I would be married again. That meant that He was trusting me to be something more now. I froze as tears welled in my eyes. God loved me enough to give me a second chance at loving someone else at a time when I was certain that I would not love again. I thought that I was destined to be alone. On top of all of that He was calling me to pastor a church!

As I left church, I just had to call someone. For whatever the reason Stella was the first person to come to mind. But it was after 9:30 pm so I texted instead. "Umm…the Apostle just gave me my reason for celebration," I would say. Her response: "Really?" I told her what Dad said and Stella said, "That's good for you, right?" Of course, this was a good thing I remember thinking. Yet, I was careful not to try to overthink this. I really did not know what to say but I managed to catch myself and reflect on what I had forfeited on my ministerial journey before now. The next text I sent read:

"Yes. Now understand that the first time that pastoral revelation was given to me I ran with it. I can admit now that I was not mature enough to handle it but that is not the case now...I fully understand the depth of the spiritual responsibility I have regarding others, like the very individual in this text thread! I have work to finish...the devil knows my name for sure, but it is time for him to bow to the NAME OF JESUS!"

My purpose was now being made crystal clear in the face of the clouds that were surrounding me. I was about to get ready for my rainy season. Which meant I was about to go through a spiritual growth spurt. God was preparing me for a place within His purpose, on in which I would have to stand firm and be immovable.

Look at 1 Corinthians 15:58 (MSG): "With all this going for us, my dear, dear friends, stand your ground. And don't hold back. Throw yourselves into the work of the Master, confident that nothing you do for him is a waste of time or effort." I was not a waste and I did not know it yet, but I was headed deep into a wasteland personally and professionally in order to bring order, structure, and clarity to people in desperate need of a victory.

As I headed home, I felt secure in God's presence. I was high on a cloud and I did not want to come down. My birthday came about the next day. There was no fanfare. It was just another day. I got one call that I did not expect in the middle of my work shift. It was from Stella. She sung an off-key version of happy birthday to me but that did not matter. What mattered was that someone cared enough to wish that upon me in the first place.

She would text a little later to ask if I was okay. I let her know that I was but something else was on my mind. I said, "Yep... taking this one moment at a time...wondering where this wife of mine is supposed to be manifesting from...but that would be getting waaaay ahead of myself...so I will just sit and wait on that one..." Stella responded, "U know I wish you the best yet to come."

It would be an uneventful night. I spent most of it in my

apartment looking at the walls. I was depressed and I knew that I needed to get out and do something. I could not just sulk. Just after 9:00 pm Stella called to see how I was. As we were on the phone I got in the car and headed out to get something to eat. I rolled around for a while and settled on Denny's. I was greeted when I walked in and told to take a seat anywhere and that someone would be with me shortly.

I am glad that Stella was on the phone right then because I would spend the next 20 minutes in the restaurant unattended. It seemed everyone around me had something interesting going on, yet I was on an island with no company present, except for who was in my ear.

We would stay on the phone past midnight just talking about random things. It did not matter what we were talking about. What mattered is that I had someone to keep me talking in the first place. Our conversation pulled me out of the depressive state I was in and kept me from occupying the same mental space that led me down that dark twisted road on December 17.

My youngest daughter turned eight on that Saturday. I was so excited because I had an opportunity to see her and her sister outside of the restrictive boundaries of the visitation center. We all had so much fun. I really enjoyed being able to see my girls in their element being their authentic selves. The birthday girl and I would take one of my favorite pictures of all time that day. I was embracing where I was and beginning to make peace with the shift that was occurring in my life. Pixie Walker says, "Self-esteem is the pillar that underlies our well-being and emotional growth." For the first time in a long time my self-esteem was somewhere other than under my feet on the floor.

Apostle Henry's obedience fell right in line with the Word in 2 Peter 1:21 (NIV): "For prophecy never had its origin in the human will, but prophets, though human, spoke from God as they were carried along by the Holy Spirit." Now on the wings of the Holy Spirit I would start to take flight, but I would be required to stand firm in my belief in Christ, accepting nothing less than His absolute best and fully trusting the promises of His Word in order to truly take off.

7

STANDING FIRM IN CONFIRMATION

As I returned home from my daughter's birthday party, I parked my car and headed to check my mail. As I did this woman who I will call Lisa said hello. I returned her courtesy. She said, "Oh, so you do actually come out of your apartment. Most times when I see you, you are always moving so quickly. I have spoken to you a couple of times but it's like you just ignored me." "I'm sorry, trust me when I tell you I just did not see you. I have had to be so focused lately on what I have had to do."

She would go on to tell me how handsome I was. She was pretty herself, but I was not really locked in on that. We ended up having a wide-ranging conversation. We talked about our journey to the present place, our children, society and our place in it as African Americans, and religion. As it was Lisa did not believe in God. As a believer myself I was intrigued as to why that was.

I figured that having an intellectual conversation about religious issues would challenge my mind, but I also relished the opportunity to let my own walk be an example of Christ's redemptive power. I could not wait to tell her the "why" of my relationship with Christ but before I could do that I listened intently.

Over the next three weeks Lisa would challenge me in ways that I had not encountered EVER! I did not back down though. Because of her I really had to walk out the Word written in 1 Peter

3:15-16: "But sanctify the Lord God in your hearts, and always *be* ready to *give* a defense to everyone who asks you a reason for the hope that is in you, with meekness and fear; having a good conscience, that when they defame you as evildoers, those who revile your good conduct in Christ may be ashamed."

I was beginning to get confused a bit because on July 30th the judge signed my divorce papers, but we were still in the 30-day moratorium period. The divorce would become final on Friday, August 3rd. In that period Lisa really took a liking to me. I liked her too but her stance on unbelief in Christ grated on me very quickly. No matter what I said about biblical truths she was determined to undermine the power of the Word. I knew with the path I was on it would not work.

Saturday morning, August 4th was a visitation day. I had enough money to get to Crossing Point to see my girls, but I really did not have enough for food and other things that I would normally do on that now bi-weekly trip. Stella, hearing my mention of this asked if I could meet her at the VA that morning. She said she would pull some money to help me out.

I met her up at the job before my trip. I was expecting $20 or $30 just to help me, which I would pay back as soon as the opportunity presented itself. She would put the money in my hand and tell me to have a safe trip. I got back to my car not knowing that she had put $100 in my hand. When I got to the car, she texted to ask me what I was thinking. I said, "Actually I just told God that if I could be half the friend you have been to me, I would be doing something." The seed she sowed was one that she did not have to, and I was appreciative. What's more, she made sure to let me know that she did NOT want me to pay it back. As I headed up the highway, I prayed that she would have a 100-fold return on her seed.

Lisa would keep coming by to talk or asking me to meet her out by the pool. I did like having company and I did enjoy talking to her, but she was NOT relaxing on where she stood with God. She was adamant that when it came to having belief in God and who He was, she just couldn't...PERIOD! Basketball great Bill Russell said, "It is far more important to understand than to be understood." In conversation with Lisa, I tried to keep that statement in mind. I must admit, though, I was getting queasy with each denial she would make, and they would get stronger as the days passed.

One evening when I was working, I had received a steam burn while operating the dish machine. The discomfort that I felt from this would not relax for a couple of days. The subsequent mark that it left upon my neck made this look more like a hickey than what it was. When I went to church one of the ministers noticed it and quietly said, "Brother, you may want to cover that passion mark on your neck..." I assured her that it was a steam burn and nothing else. After hearing that, she would help me apply some makeup over that area so that I would not give the wrong idea to others in the church.

This would not be the only time that this blemish would come into question though. The next day at work when Stella first saw me, she was feeling some type of way, but she kept that to herself and did not disclose those thoughts to me. When we spoke, she said, "Tre, did you and Lisa hook up?" "No," I said, as I tried to figure out why she was asking me the question. Remembering the mark on my neck I continued as I pointed to it saying, "Oh, that is a steam burn. At this point I wish it would have been a hickey, at least then it would not burn as bad." As I laughed, Stella would manage a weak "Oh, okay..."

As she would tell me much later, she had been relieved that Lisa and I had not hooked up and that the mark on my neck was not what she first thought it was. Upon realizing this she was confused. How she was feeling really did not make sense because she was still in a relationship with her baby's father. Soon after those thoughts would leave her mind, though she could not shake the fact that she had the thought in the first place. Throughout the course of Stella and I's conversations during this time I continued to wonder out loud who this wife was that was being sent to me. In one instance she would say in response to my inquiry, "It's me isn't it?" I paused and then said, "No friend, I cannot say that. If you were you would be the first to know. Wait, actually, you would be the third because God would know, then He would tell me so that I could then tell you." Her question was interesting though because she just blurted it out...

Lisa and I were having a decent conversation one night and had been talking for a while out on my balcony when religion came back up as a topic. At one critical point Lisa flat out disrespected God and the vitriol that she did this with had me incensed! I told her that she was going to have to leave and that after this I would not be able to talk to her anymore.

Confused by my response, Lisa would ask, "Is there someone else?" This question confused me because we were not actually together, but I gave her an answer, nonetheless. I said, "Yes, God and His Son." "I wasn't talking about Him, she said." "Well, I am. Yet and still, I will NOT deny Him and will not let people close to me who do. I have my daughters. I have to continue living right for them." Her voice had deepened now, as she said, "No, is there another FEMALE?" I needed these interactions to be over! My response had turned very stern by now as I said, "You know what? Yes, there IS! With you, if we ever hooked up, I would end up empty because we cannot be connected spiritually. With this other person, I would never have to worry about that because we already are connected spiritually." The look in my eyes would change as I continued, "I do NOT have to apologize for the call and anointing that is on my life because not only does she understand it, she embraces it!"

Lisa was not taking this "NO" for an answer! She kept pressing. Amid all of this I was gathering the dishes that she had let me borrow so that I could be sure that she would not have any reason to interact with me moving forward. I gave her back her dishes. She was pissed, stormed out, and slammed my door. There would be no more distractions from her moving forward, I was moving on.

The next morning, I texted Stella and let her know that "Whatever would or could have been with Lisa won't be...I let her know that I couldn't deal with her anymore." As I let Stella know the details, she would say, "Good for you..." Solid in my convictions I would go on to say, "I know I did the right thing there. Someone out there is truly made for me in this season. I just have to continue to let God do His work..." Even with the prophecy now in place I was taking the confession a step further by calling the things that were not as if they were (see Romans 4:17).

I was still a bit perplexed as to the person who was to come out of the prophecy that had been spoken. Lisa was not that ONE, so I was trying to keep my focus. Yet, in another conversation, Stella would ask again, "It's me isn't it?" I could not give her the firm answer because I still did not know for myself and I was not trying to misplay this and get out of step with God.

A couple of days later I would start to understand the depth of the feelings that I was beginning to feel for her. That Sunday morning, I went to church. I texted Stella a couple of times, the last one asking how her day was. But she did not respond all day. At 11:30 pm I started pressing in for her and interceding on her behalf because I had not heard anything from her. I was deeply concerned, and that concern would remain well into the next day.

Finally, just after noon I would hear from her letting me know she was okay via text. When I saw that, I was adamant in my response saying, "Ok. DO NOT scare me like that again, okay! I've been pressed in prayer for you since 11:30 last night!!!" In finding out that Stella was alright, I started to find out that there may be something more there. Initially, I was deeply concerned for my friend. Through intercession and pleading with God I came to see that the world as I now knew it would not be the same if she was not in it. She was the one friend that I had in the local area and being that it took me awhile to find a confidant who could help me make some sense of the happenings in my life, not hearing from her for that space of time hurt.

I have lost a lot in my life and had my share of heartbreak. That heartbreak coupled with that same thing which I directly caused had me appreciating where I now was. I was having a now deep and personal experience of getting to know my friend, but I could not figure out exactly what it was supposed to mean. Robin Roberts paints the picture of my dilemma here brilliantly when she says, "Life provides losses and heartbreak for all of us-but the greatest tragedy is to have the experience and miss the meaning."

I was given new life with Dad's prophecy, but I was not sure if I was gaining the true measure of what was supposed to be coming with it. Tom Bodett writes, "The difference between school and life? In school, you're taught a lesson and then given a test. In life, you're given a test that teaches you a lesson." Now, it was not about learning lessons, I was trying to make sure that I was able to apply what I learning as I continued to move forward. But I could not shake the fact that these feelings I was having, coupled with the circumstances that surrounded them, had left me profoundly confused.

God is always a steady and present companion to us, if we allow Him to be. I had lost sight of Him on my path before and that was my own fault because I tried to walk by myself through valleys that I created. This time was different, and I needed it to be. I turned to the book of Isaiah to find a clear reminder of this. Isaiah 41:13 (NLT) says, "For I hold you by your right hand— I, the LORD your God. And I say to you, 'Don't be afraid. I am here to help you." I was starting to walk in light, and I was not about to let go.

Monday August 20th God opened the floodgates and in the overflow of that waterfall He brought the clarity that I had been seeking. I had a flat tire that morning and while getting it fixed in the parking lot of my apartment complex I ran into Lisa. She was angry when she saw me and began to hurl all these accusations at me, saying that I was a false prophet and that God wasn't in me. During her roughly two-minute profanity laced tirade all I could do was smile.

Somewhere during this attack, I began to drown out what she was saying. It sounded something like Charlie Brown's teacher in all those cartoons. But my smile kept getting bigger! All I could think about was Stella. Amid all that was happening God said, "Tre, she IS your wife and when it comes to Stella LaVin DO NOT put me in a box." I had my answer but now I had to make the phone call. As much as I wanted to be able to tell her this in person, God told me to tell her and do it right then. So, as I headed to work, I started dialing.

Stella was at work, but she was able to pick up. I asked how she was doing and told her that she would not believe who I just ran into. I told her that God was starting to make some things clear and explained what had just happened with Lisa. I wanted to tell her what God said but I was taking my time to get there because I was not sure what she would say. I KNEW what God said but would she agree? I did not know. Somewhere during this exchange Stella just blurted out, **"I'm the one, I'm your wife???"** It was not as much a question as it was some greater form of confirmation.

After a deep breath I said, "Yes, sweetheart you are the one. You are my wife! One thing though…I was SUPPOSED to be the one to tell you what God said but you are always blurting out something, so you beat me to it." SILENCE! About 45 seconds passed before either one of us said anything. We needed some time to let that sink in. Then we both laughed at the same time. We would not really be able to talk face-to-face at work, so we continued our conversation via text once I reported inside.

As I arrived inside the department, I was trying to catch my breath from what had been a whirlwind. By confirming the prophecy spoken by Apostle Henry, God was reminding me of the power of His Word written in Isaiah 55:11 which says, "So shall My word be that goes forth from My mouth; It shall not return to Me void, But it shall accomplish what I please, And it shall prosper in the thing for which I sent it." My marching orders were now issued, and I had to step up and claim what God said was rightfully mine. Confirmation kept coming as the next scripture I was reminded of came quickly from Jeremiah 29:11 (NIV): "For I know the plans I have for you," declares the LORD, "plans to prosper you and not to harm you, plans to give you hope and a future."

With God being firmly in control I knew this could not be bad. Any questions I had to that point came about because I was not sure of my future, let alone God's plan for it. He had a plan laid out for me to prosper. As much as my incarceration, divorce, and brokenness had forced me to own my past and take responsibility for it, I now had to own my future, and the plan for prosperity and hope that came with it.

As Stella and I continued our conversation through text she asked, "You sure u want a divorce?" (Never mind it was already finalized). My answer was one that I did not have to think about and in it I was clear, strong, and direct. I said,

> "I ain't going backward Hun. I KNOW what God has said! My children will always be protected, and my ex-wife will always have a special place in my heart but it's time to walk fully in God's purpose for me, one that now includes YOU Dear!"

She had a simple response: "It's unbelievable." I then continued:

> "You need to know that I look forward now with no regret or blame on myself because of what God has done to restore me...and if I didn't transition through some of those valleys, I wouldn't have met you in the first place! Divine appointment is a wonderful thing."

Again, her response was simple: Yeah, it's a wonderful thang." But then I had a serious question for her. I said, "So, the next question is are you willing to prepare to be the one?" She said, "Whatever God wants, it's not about me. He knows what's best for me, better than I know what is best for myself. It's not about me."

Her point was a good one, but I probed still a bit deeper. I said, "This is so true. But one still must want to be obedient, which is why I asked. In this case it takes both of us to say yes to His plan..." "Yes," she would say. Confirming what I was asking I said, "Yes Lord I will do this. I need my heart and mind to get to the same place because one has been fluttering all day." With that, Stella and I were officially a couple.

Stella's self-esteem before she met me had been extremely low. She did not think much of herself and she had a hard time seeing the beautiful truths about herself that were so obvious to other people around her. Knowing this, I started to make a point each day to try to get her to see herself in a different light, one that would not only give her confidence, but one that would help her build it. I remember telling her she was amazing, and she asked me why I said that. I gave her a loose definition off the top of my head, reminding her that she was someone who not only took my breath away and left me speechless but that she also made my heart melt. Upon hearing what I said, she was left speechless…

A while back I had asked Stella if she had a bible. She said she did. I asked her what kind and she said she had a basic one. I knew that she was going to need a true study bible so that she would be fully equipped to walk in her purpose alongside me. Over the next couple of days, I would make it my mission to make sure that she had one.

We had spent a lot of time getting to know each other through phone calls, texts, and work but we had yet to see each other outside the work environment. We settled on meeting up on Sunday August 26th in Hallmark where she lived. As it were, she lived 36 minutes away from me but that did not matter. She was now a major piece of my destiny assignment so whatever the distance I knew that God would make a way and redeem the time.

I met Stella after church about a mile from her house at the gas station. From there we would head out to the mall. When she pulled up and got out of her car, I was instantly excited. This would be the first time that I would be able to give her a true hug outside of work. As she took a seat in my car, I let her know that I had something for her.

I gave her the bag and she started to go through it. Her serious look turned to a smile as she pulled out the bible that I had gotten for her. I wrote this message inside it for her,

> "Stella, I cannot think of a more important gift to give you than this sword which will equip you for every battle you will ever face. By the Word in Esther 4:14 embrace this very moment for which you were created. May your walk with God always be fruitful! His love always – Tre – 8/26"

Ester 4:14 (NIV) reads: "For if you remain silent at this time, relief and deliverance for the Jews will arise from another place, but you and your father's family will perish. And who knows but that you have come to your royal position for such a time as this?" I needed her to concentrate on the "b" section of the verse.

We headed to the mall and had a great time just laughing and having a free-flowing conversation. Stella did not want to be out too long because she had to go and purchase school clothes for her children as they were due to start school the next day. As I was dropping her back off at her car she asked if I wanted to meet her at the store to give her time to go pick up her children. I told her I did not mind. We would meet at Burlington Coat Factory near her house.

Stella's were children were 20, 15, 10, 5, and 3 years old, respectively. The younger four were still living at home with her. They came into the store and she introduced us. Her five-year-old is autistic and the first thing he wanted to do was rub the top of my head and get on my shoulders. I lifted him up and we would spend most of the next 30 minutes establishing a connection.

Her oldest son stayed to himself and did not say too much as he was more focused on putting outfits that he liked together. Her youngest daughter was shy at first, but she would warm up throughout our time together in the store. The biggest connection would be made however, with her 10-year-old son. The entire time we were in the store he followed me around and could not stop smiling.

When it was time to go, I walked Stella and the kids to their car. Her ten-year old asked where I was about to go but before I could answer he said, "Mom can he come with us?" Stella and I had not discussed this, but he did not care. She hesitated but said it was okay. Her son was so excited he invited himself to ride with me, which I did not have a problem with. Her son and I rode to their house together and cracked jokes the entire way. Once we arrived, we entered the house through the garage. Stella felt weird because she had not had the opportunity to clean the house before she left. That did not matter to me though. I was just honored to be invited over in the first place. Being able to look around gave me an opportunity to see what kind of help she may need moving forward.

I did not stay long because I knew that the kids had school the next day. Plus, it was really our first date and I did not want to disrespect her house in any way. But I really enjoyed being around them and getting this opportunity to spend time with Stella outside of work.

Stella asked the next day at work if I wanted to stop by for a little bit after I got off and spend some time. I let her know that I would be honored. When my shift ended, I stopped home to shower and then I made the 36-minute trip across town. I arrived just after 8:30 pm.

As the kids readied themselves for bed Stella and I continued to talk. As she went to her room, I maintained my distance on the floor. After a few minutes Stella said that I was welcome to stay because it was getting late and she was worried about me having to drive back across town. I agreed to stay. As the kids were heading off to school the next morning and Stella was readying for work her 10-year-old asked, "Mr. Tre, when are you coming back?"

Once again, Stella and I had not discussed this. But to my surprise she said, "Yeah Tre, that is a good question..." Both of their looks turned serious. I thought for a moment and responded, "Well, I guess I can come back tonight if you all will have me..." "That's fine, Stella would say." As it turns out I would come back that next night and except for one night to come moving forward I would not leave again. I had no clue that with what lay ahead how very important that decision would come to be.

8

Family and Spinal Fusions

I must admit it felt a little strange being in this new environment after having been alone for the two and a half years previous. I was both excited and relieved. Excited to have someone who wanted to have me around every day and relieved because I was about to need an entirely different type of support.

The pain in my neck was not getting any better. It was getting increasingly more difficult to perform my essential job functions without noticeable pain. My body had stopped responding favorably to occupational therapy and I was highly discouraged. With no other relief in sight and most other remedies not achieving the desired results surgery was recommended.

A procedure called an anterior cervical discectomy and fusion (ACDF) was recommended for me. This procedure is used to remove herniated or degenerative discs in the neck and can also be used to decompress nerves. Being that I had a pinched nerve and a herniated disc with degenerative disc disease this would allow me a strong prognosis for recovery and a decent quality of life moving forward. The disc itself would be replaced with a titanium graft which would help to fuse my spine together and eventually help to alleviate the deep pain I had been experiencing. It was a risk but any path to relief had to be better than constant, lingering and escalating discomfort. The doctors informed me of the risks that were involved, which included possible infection and more permanent damage to the nerve root itself.

There would be another set of concerns that could literally affect a different call of mine. "Mr. LaVin, you would not happen to be a preacher or a singer, would you?" the nurse would ask. "I am actually both of those" I said. "Well, I just have to let you know that there are roughly ten percent of people who do not regain their talking or singing voices after surgery," he would go on to say.

I had to acknowledge what I was hearing, and I did, but I chose to call on a more certain truth to help me here. In response I said, "You say ten percent, huh? That may be a fact but let me tell you the TRUTH...the truth is that God will restore me to health and heal my wounds!" (see Jeremiah 30:17) When the nurse saw the conviction that rested on my face and the calm demeanor with which I said the statement he said, "You know what? No argument here...let's go with that!" Surgery would be scheduled for Monday October 29th.

In the meantime, I was preparing to meet Stella's mother, Allison, for the first time. She would be coming to stay with us for a couple of weeks while she was continuing her treatments for stage four kidney cancer at the cancer center in Horne. She had these appointments every two months or so. She would arrive on September 15th. I was excited to meet her, but I knew at some point I was going to have to tell her the truth about my past. I was not afraid to do that because I knew that if we were going to have any form of a relationship it would have to be built on trust and honesty.

A few days into her visit, she would finally ask about my divorce and why it happened. Just as I had done with her daughter, I told her the entire truth. It caught her off guard a little bit, but she appreciated the fact that I was honest with her. In letting me know how much respect she had gained for me she only had two requests, "take care of my daughter and don't hurt my grandchildren," she would say. Those were two asks that I could deal with, so I readily agreed. Yet, just as Stella, her mother, and I were beginning to find our footing news would come that would rock the foundation of the family and change our lives in an instant.

Monday, September 24th started as a normal day. It was my parents wedding anniversary and I called them that morning to congratulate them and wish them well. Stella had been in some pain and asked her baby's father if he could bring her some pain medication up to the job. She met him in the parking lot, told him thank you, and went back to work.

Stella and I were returning home when she got a phone call from a number that she did not recognize. While she wondered who was calling her, she did not really pay it any mind. When they called right back, she answered. After she said hello the inflection in her voice changed almost immediately. "Wait, what?!? Slow down," she would say...then she screamed, "No, what about my baby?" All the kids that lived with her were either in the car or already at home so I was trying to figure out who she could be talking about. By now she was screaming and inconsolable.

As she got out of the car with tears in her eyes she said, "He died. Do you know who?" "No," I would say, still trying to figure out who she was talking about. She pointed at her youngest daughter and said, "Her dad..." By now her oldest son was in the garage. "Go get your grandmother," I managed to say. When her mom came outside, Stella gave her the news. Both would collapse into my arms. The screams were piercing.

It did not matter that their relationship had ended, what mattered was that the father of one of Stella's children was now gone...without warning! One reality hit her quickly, "Tre, she doesn't have a father," she would say, her voice trailing off...I did not hesitate with my response, "She does now." It did not matter that we were not married yet. I knew what I was supposed to do. What did matter was that even though this little girl had just lost her father, God put me right where I was supposed to be to ensure that she would not grow up without one.

The next couple of hours were a blur. We headed across town to the hospital to meet up with his family. We were told that he had a massive heart attack. However, the details that surrounded everything were still very sketchy at best. Amid this news and seeing Stella's face and demeanor I let her know that I would not be going to work the next day. I was going to be certain that she did not go through this by herself. Work for me would have to wait and it was the furthest thing from my mind.

We arrived at the hospital trying to get some answers but there were not too many available. Stella wanted to see if she could see him, but they had already moved him to the hospital's morgue. With the family visibly shaken, God gave me words of encouragement for them. I did not know any of them but that did not matter either. While I do not remember most of what was said I do remember offering hope through the following scripture in Psalm 116:15, which reminds that, "Precious in the sight of the Lord is the death of His saints."

As we returned home, I just tried to be present for Stella and her children. Not much would be said, and very little sleep was had be anyone that night. The situation would be very cloudy over the next couple of weeks, but I was sure of one thing: I was NOT supposed to move. Whatever it would take for me to be there for them and assist during this time I was going to do so.

A cookout and gathering was held at a place the family called "The Berm" that Saturday. I drove Stella to this function and would be introduced as her co-worker and friend who was a pastor and knew how to deal with things in times like this. That was fine with me. I did not say much, I just tried to do the one thing I could do at that time, which was be there for Stella and her daughter. The following Saturday, October 6th was his funeral. I would not be able to attend the actual service because I had visitation with my girls, and I could not miss that. I did, however, make sure that Stella and her daughter got to the funeral home and once there I paid my respects.

I was torn, knowing that I wanted and had to see my girls, but I wanted to be there for Stella too. Being that I could not be in two places simultaneously, my emotions were all over the place. As I drove back from visitation I waited for Stella's call. I just wanted to know how she was holding up. When I did hear from her, she let me know that it had been a long day but that she was okay. Hearing this, I felt a little bit better, but I knew going forward that there was a hole in two hearts that I would not ever be able to fill.

By now, I was just over three weeks away from having surgery and was told that I should expect to miss about five weeks of work while I recovered. In the meantime, I went to work, still in pain, but thankful that some relief would come in the coming days, much sooner, at this point, than later.

While it is true that there was a lot of heaviness trying to deal with what was and with what was to come, I was about to achieve another milestone that I had been diligently working toward. The date and ceremony to commemorate my becoming licensed in the state to preach was upon me.

Stella's thirst and zeal for the Lord was being rewarded too and she would walk with me and be acknowledged as a ministerial aspirant, which meant that while she was not being licensed yet, she would be upon completion of her ministry schooling. I was proud to be accomplishing this, but I was also extremely honored to be able to share the moment with her.

The ceremony took place on Sunday October 21st. I had nervous energy that morning because I was thankful and appreciate of what God was allowing to happen for me. This was another area that He was trusting me in, and I just wanted to be sure, once again that I was honoring Him the right way. It just proves that when God has something for you it truly is for you no one can take it away. Revelation 3:7-9 (MSG) says,

> "Write this to Philadelphia, to the Angel of the church. The Holy, the True—David's key in his hand, opening doors no one can lock, locking doors no one can open—speaks: "I see what you've done. Now see what *I've* done. I've opened a door before you that no one can slam shut. You don't have much strength, I know that; you used what you had to keep my Word. You didn't deny me when times were rough. "And watch as I take those who call themselves true believers but are nothing of the kind, pretenders whose true membership is in the club of Satan—watch as I strip off their pretensions and they're forced to acknowledge it's you that I've loved."

Thank God At Rock Bottom, Jesus Was The Rock That I Hit!

What a mandate given by the Lord. When you are faithful to the Word God will reward you. The little physical strength that I had I did indeed use to do the best I could to honor Him and His Word. This ceremony and the path to it showed me that not only did I have God's approval but that He also had given me the proper equipment to walk out His true call and destiny for me. Rick Warren says, "Your life isn't an accident. You have a destiny, one that only you can complete." The tangible evidence was now manifesting itself and I was glad that I was alive to see it.

Knowing that I was going to need some help after surgery with my recovery my mother flew in from Colorado to help. Even as she did, she would get the opportunity to see my ministerial journey come full circle.

Even though the ministerial licensing ceremony had taken place already the licenses were not able to be printed in time, so we got those the following Sunday, the day before my surgery. When I got ordained to preach back in 2012 my mother could not make it, but my dad was there. Now that I was being licensed my mom was there, while my dad could not make it. Even more exciting for me was the fact that my mom would be meeting Stela for the first time.

The future was really starting look bright. But I could not get too far ahead of myself. Winston Churchill stated, "It is a mistake to try to look too far ahead. The chain of destiny can only be grasped on link at a time." I would be taking this advice very literally as one of the links in my cervical spinal chain was about to be removed and rebuilt.

The morning of surgery the doctor told me that early on, the whole of my spine would have a strange reaction to this foreign piece that was infringing on the party, trying to fit in. He said eventually the titanium would be accepted, fuse together with the other vertebrae, and end up becoming a strong, valuable member of the family. But until that happened both I and my spine were going to be reminded that there was some foreign matter in there being forced in with some jagged screws which were necessary but would not feel very good.

I would be in surgery for about four hours. When I woke up my mother was there, and I remember feeling extremely stiff.

She told me not to try to move just yet but instead to get my bearings and feel my body out. That worked for a little while but when a portion of my neck began to itch, I tried to move, and I paid for it. I had experienced physical pain before, but this was in another zip code altogether! What made it worse was that the anesthesia had not worn off yet!

Not too long after the anesthesia wore off Stella came up to visit which was not difficult to do because I was being treated in the very hospital where we both worked, and our department was in the basement. It felt good to see her. Had this surgery happened even a few months earlier I very well may have been having to recover on my own with no help from anyone.

It is interesting the simple things we take for granted in life! Raising both my hands above my head to praise and worship the Lord was something that I had not been able to do in full for a long time because of the pain that was constant on my right side. After some more time passed, I was able to lift both my arms and keep them up in praise to the Lord and when I did there was NO PAIN! As tears welled in my eyes, I has Stella take a picture so that I could have record of that very moment.

When you have a spinal fusion like the one I had they make about a two-inch incision in the front of your neck to have an easier point of access to the spine itself. They split the muscle and move your trachea and esophagus as well This is all well and fine, that is, until you must eat!

I found out very quickly that I would have to learn how to swallow all over again. My gag reflex was overactive and that caused my food to boomerang itself back upward, leading me to have to ease it, though forcibly, back down. Over the next two weeks even though I would be hungry I could not finish more than half of any meal because it hurt too much to swallow. This also made taking my medications damn near impossible because I had to take each of the 8-13 pills prescribed one at a time over the jagged runway that now lay in my throat. You would think that I could have gotten at least *some* of these meds in liquid form, but this is me we are talking about so I should have known that part would not be easy!

I got discharged from the hospital on the next afternoon

and headed home. I would not be able to drive for about five weeks though and that meant that I would miss two visits with my daughters. I understood why that had to be, but it did not make that pain any better.

I have always been a very physically active person so to have to literally bring everything to a crawl was difficult for me to adjust to. I was told that I could not lift more than ten pounds and I really had to let others help me do things. My mind would see what I needed to do just as clear as day, but my body would be so far behind.

To walk from room to room would seem to take five to ten minutes at any given time. Laying down hurt. Standing up hurt. Sitting still hurt. At some point I thought that I was being tricked. I remember telling my mom, "I thought they said I was supposed to be getting better? "And you will," she would say, "It's just going to take some time."

Stella's youngest had a birthday coming up. Even though I could not move around very well I wanted to do what I could to help make her day special being that she had just lost her dad. Stella said that her daughter really liked Chuck E. Cheese so that is where we took her and her other siblings to. She and her siblings had a really good time and I was certainly glad to see that.

Stella's birthday was coming up also. She told me that she did not really do anything to celebrate and that it was just another day. It would not be just another day for me, and I was determined to make it a time she would not only want to remember but would not soon be able to forget.

While all these things were happening, we were all trying to adjust to me being in the house. Stella, having been a single mother for many years before meeting me was set in a routine. Her children, especially her two oldest sons, were not only very overprotective of their mom but extremely jealous that she was starting to pay attention and give love to someone other than them.

I am extremely organized and thrive very well in structured environments with routines. Stella, on the other hand, is extremely laid back and likes to do some things without having to plan them, fearful that everything may not go like it was planned when the time comes.

I was doing my best to try to fit in with everybody in the house, but I was trying too hard. With the way my life had shifted everything was new and nothing I was experiencing was familiar. Stella and her kids were very settled into their routines and had trouble adjusting to not only the structure I tried to provide but the discipline as well.

There was not much I could really say on that front. After all, I was an invited guest in their home, even though Stella and I were in a relationship and nothing there, outside of my clothes and vehicle belonged to me. I knew I was sent to help Stella and her kids, but they did not see my help as "help" they saw most of what I did as an annoying form of nagging.

Understand this. Stella did, indeed, give God a specific list of things she wanted in a relationship with a man. She did not want him to be a person who tripped and gave her trouble. She wanted him to physically be able to take care of himself. She wanted someone who did not treat her bad, especially given all the emotional abuse she had already endured. She wanted someone who was not jealous, and she wanted support.

Even as she asked God for all these things, Stella did not expect Him to answer her so quickly. She thought she would have more time. Matter of fact, she was okay if it never happened. She was fully prepared for a life that just involved her and her children. This way she would not have to worry about a man who was not the children's father giving her trouble about her children. She got the man she was asking for, in me, within a matter of *weeks* and it literally caught her off guard, right along with her kids.

As we all tried our best to get comfortable with each other I was literally turning out to be just like the new piece of titanium in my spine. While I was trying to fuse and align with the family there were reminders everywhere that I was completely different than anything or anyone that they had ever been used to.

Even amid all the growing pains and adjustments I truly believed that there was absolutely no place I would rather be than right there with them. I had been lonely and alone before and I was not about to prove God wrong by running away from this family just because everything was not ready made to fall right into place.

9

DESTINY FULFILLED

Dictionary.com defines the verb fulfill this way: "to carry out, or bring to realization, as a prophecy or promise." Stella and I were talking about houses one night and during the conversation I started to think how special it would be to have her realize her dream of home ownership. As I was listening to her I remember thinking, "Dear God, if there is a way to make this possible for them, make a way and show me. I will be obedient to not only what you say but how you tell me to do it."

Stella had asked what the area that I had my apartment in was like for schools. I told her that I did not really know but that I would do some research. When I started to investigate this God let me know the area in Horne that she asked me about was not where we were supposed to be.

I had one major concern. As a father who was not able to see his own children except under extremely strict stipulations, I did not want to move the children away from their father. They were going to need him as they continued to grow, and I wanted to ensure they had not only the opportunity but especially the access that would allow them to be their absolute best as they grew up. The principle itself was too important to me and I could not be the one responsible for pulling kids from their father, especially on my own, apart from God.

It does not take much to please or impress Stella. Since day one I had been paying attention to the things that she liked and had started getting some small things together that I would present to her spread out over the course of the week of her birthday, which was also the same week as Thanksgiving.

There were devotional books, a candle, a Jesus themed t-shirt, and lotions from a popular specialty store. Lastly, there was her engagement ring which we had already picked out the month prior, along with my wedding band. So, the surprise would not be if she would be getting married, as God gave us that answer, but rather when I would propose.

Stella really likes to eat at a restaurant called Pepper's. I wanted to take her somewhere a little more elegant and formal for her actual birthday, but she insisted that she did not need all that. So, to end her birthday "week" I at least knew where we would go. However, before we could get there, God started talking to me about legacies.

I wanted to start putting down seed that would not only last but would be watered in a way that allowed Stella and her children to prosper and grow. I wanted to show them that good things were possible for them too and that they truly did deserve good things to happen to them in their own lives.

I knew how important it was to not only leave an inheritance for your children's children (see Proverbs 13:22) but to build a steady bridge to it as well. I did not just want to leave the world behind, I wanted to embody what Benjamin Disraeli said when he stated, "The legacy of heroes is the memory of a great name and the inheritance of a great example." I had set enough bad examples before, why not do something worthwhile to change that and leave something that all my children could be proud to emulate?

To give you some context, I was doing something that was not popular, and a lot of men made sure I knew it. Everyone from Apostle Henry on down had concerns about me being in a relationship with a woman who had **five** kids. "Son, are you sure that you are ready to do that? I know she is a wonderful lady but that is a lot of responsibility," the Apostle would say. "Man, there ain't no way I would raise someone else's kids, let alone five of them," someone else said. The theme was the same.

I was not interested in doing something that other people

Thank God At Rock Bottom, Jesus Was The Rock That I Hit!

wanted to do and I certainly did not appreciate the fact that they were trying to project onto me what they would **NOT** do. If God said it, I was going to do it and that was the end of the discussion as far as I was concerned! God made sure I did not take my own life for a purpose; HIS purpose, and I knew that I was now in a position to speak life into people who felt like there was not anything great in store for their own lives. Establishing a place of our own for Stella and me with the kids was important to our growth and I wanted to be sure I was walking in obedience.

The week of November 18th through 24th I began to give Stella the small gifts one-by-one. I would give her one gift each day until Friday and then take her to dinner and propose on Saturday, which was her birthday. She was excited to be getting these gifts. The smile on her face was truly priceless! When she received her t-shirt on Thanksgiving Day, she was so excited. She said joyfully, "Can I put this on right now???" I told her that she could, and she kept looking at it all throughout the rest of the day.

Friday came and we would go looking at houses in our local area. We got out and looked around a subdivision just down the street from Stella's house. The houses in there were nice but it was not anything that really drew our attention. There were some new houses being built in the subdivision where we were living, and Stella wanted to look at some of those. We saw a couple of layouts that we liked. As we were driving around, we drove past the housing office.

As I doubled back toward the office, I told Stella to stay in the car. "I am just going to ask them how much these homes are going for, I'll be right back," I said. When I got inside, I asked the sales representative a few questions. When I finished, I let him know that I had my girlfriend in the car. "Bring her in if you want, you both can feel free to walk through the model home right here." "Couldn't hurt, let me get her," I told him. When I told Stella to get out and come inside, she was confused. "The man said we could come take a look inside," I said.

She followed me inside and we introduced ourselves. After looking around and liking what we saw the man asked if we wanted to run a credit check to see where we stood. With my divorce now a few months past being final I did want to see what my credit looked like, so we agreed to let him run the credit check. The result would surprise us both.

Stella had never owned her own home before. Being that I was a military Veteran I had already used VA loans to purchase four homes previously. Initially, we had been looking in a price range but when the representative told us what we could be approved for it shocked me. I did not think that I could be approved for as much as he said, especially with that amount being a full $100,000 over the price range we had been looking in.

I had planned a wide range of things for this special week already but signing a contract on a home had not been one of those. What made this even more improbable was that this house would be built from the ground up. This meant that Stella and I could walk into something that was uniquely ours.

Stella had one request. "Tre, I want this to be a surprise for the kids, so I don't want to tell them until we are about to move in," she said. The idea sounded good to me so I told her that would not be a problem at all. Stella really could not believe what happened. She kept asking me, "Tre, are you sure you didn't plan this?" Since I did not plan this my answer was a simple, "No, I promise you I didn't." With how well this thing came together I was shocked at God's efficiency myself.

Stella had to work the next day, her birthday. When she got home and freshened up, her and I headed to Pepper's. We were seated and we ordered our food. I had the engagement ring in my medicine bag because the box was too big to put inside any of my pockets.

Before desert I excused myself to go to the bathroom. I planned to text Stella a message, but I would not send it to her until right before I made it back to the table. Once she started reading it, I would be on my knee waiting to propose. The plan was simple, but Stella did not cooperate fully on her end. Instead of reading the message completely from the beginning she only read the end of it, the part where I asked, "Will you marry me?"

She read the question correctly but something in her brain did not quite register what I asked. By now, I was on bended knee asking her the question for the second time. In her shock, Stella forgot to answer. The look of confusion was followed by complete joy and then, finally, she managed to say, "Yes." I slipped the ring on her finger and then watched as she put her hands on her face in amazement. Somehow, I was able to pull off this surprise. All week she would have NO clue what I was up to. In that moment I took another of my favorite pictures ever. This would be the perfect cap to what was a wonderful week. The prophecy was spoken a few months prior but now, the foundation of what it would take to walk it out was being laid in concrete!

I was getting close to returning to work. I had missed just under four weeks and I was gaining some of my strength back. But a different level of strength was about to be tested. Though my paperwork requesting leave under the Federal Medical Leave Act (FMLA) had been submitted back in June my department dragged their feet on getting it approved. I had been in communication weekly with my administrative personnel but still did not have a firm answer on the approval of my leave. Up to now this had not been an issue because I had enough leave on the books to still draw a check and I could lean on my VA entitlement as well.

I would return to work on Monday December 3rd. It felt good to be back at work, but I did not feel like myself. I was still on a ten-pound weight lift limit and to make matters worse I had a place to work on the schedule, but my bosses had overlooked me and put someone else in my same spot. So, even though I was physically back at work, I was there without an actual place to "be." I was working but I was being hardheaded. I kept trying to do the things my mind knew to do but my body was not ready to fully execute certain tasks.

With me recovering at home over the previous few weeks and with the way the work schedule fell, Stella and I had not been able to attend church. We had grown increasingly frustrated with this development. Stella was also trying to get some paperwork from the church that she could give to her supervisors at work so she could attend school full time over the next six months. It seemed like everything kept getting in the way whenever the time came to produce that paperwork.

When we finally did make it to church on Wednesday December 12th Stella and I were weighed down and it showed.

During the sermon Dad knew something was off and would call me out to refocus but the news I had just received had me pissed and I was not able to hide it. My leave and earnings statement (LES) had been emailed to let me know how much money would be deposited into my back account that coming Friday. It read: NET Pay: $186.84. I had to look at that again. Then I showed Stella and I had to look at the number one more time. It was right. My department had dropped the ball at work. I had expected $1086. I was beside myself, "How could people be so irresponsible. This would now affect my household and I needed answers!

When service ended, Apostle Henry asked to see Stella and me. We sat down and told him what was going on. He said, "Come on now, Son, as a man of God, you know that the attack is coming, I can't have you fold up your tent now!" I was still fuming when I said, "I fully understand that Dad, but I'm not going to sit up here and be fake either!" "Come on, Son, I need you. Stay in the fight. I NEED you! Dad needs you next to me, Son, to complete this work," he pleaded.

It was clear that the purpose of us being at the church had been for that prophecy to not only be spoken but also fulfilled. The seeds had been planted. We had been tilling the ground diligently. Now it was time for us to walk out the faith steps, one by one! Word of Life had been great to us but as the needs of our family changed, we decided to move on.

We were about to be in the throws of deep transition but once again, I knew, without a doubt, that there was no one I would rather be running this race with than Stella, and therefore, no place I would rather be amid the storm.

About transition Nikki Giovanni said, "A lot of people resist transition and therefore never allow themselves to enjoy who they are. Embrace the change, no matter what it is; once you do, you can learn about the new world you're in and take advantage of it."

The year 2018 was all about transitions for me. The new me was far from perfect but I stood up to be counted and that meant I was present. Walking in the present I was about to put a bow on the greatest gift God had given me this side of my rock bottom season. That gift was one of acceptance.

Thank God At Rock Bottom, Jesus Was The Rock That I Hit!

God had loved me through it all, now it was up to me to carry the mantle forward. Just as God had done with me, I would tell Stella this, "At your best, at your worst, and everywhere in between, you are loved!" Stella and I would finish the year strong. Questions had been answered and more importantly on Saturday January 12, our wedding day, God's destiny was fulfilled with no fanfare, just me, Stella, her four youngest children, and the Justice of the Peace.

We could have done this wedding big. In fact, I told Stella that she deserved a big wedding and that she had earned the right to walk down her isle of happiness. That is not what she wanted though. We had chosen the date at random by looking at the calendar in the Justice of the Peace's office once we applied and paid for the marriage license. There was only one stipulation that I put on a Saturday wedding date and that was that it could not be one a 1st or 3rd Saturday because I still had to keep my appointment to see my daughters. My daughters were not at the ceremony and I did miss them. But they knew that I was happy, and I had already told them about their step siblings.

As the ceremony started, I told the judge that I needed to present her with another set of rings. I let her know about Stella's youngest child losing her father and I told her that I had to do something special. Stella's daughter asked me one day in church if I could be her daddy. Being that she had asked me that question I took time during the ceremony to ask her if she could be my daughter. I "married" two beautiful people that day and officially gained new life and the LaVin family name had new meaning. In finding a wife I really did find a treasure and a good thing (see Proverbs 18:22).

After the ceremony we all went to Baskin Robbins and had ice cream. We all had experienced something new in becoming a family. We had all been renewed and set free. No more do overs!

> "Don't hold together what must fall apart. The familiar life crumbles so the new life can begin."
> ~ Bryant H. McGill

"We must let go of the life we have planned, so as to accept the one that is waiting for us." ~ Joseph Campbell

"Don't try to make your old life better. Allow your new life to come in. It is what you truly deserve." ~ Roxana Jones

"Because of the LORD's great love, we are not consumed, for his compassions never fail. They are new every morning; great is your faithfulness. I say to myself, "The LORD is my portion; therefore, I will wait for him." The LORD is good to those whose hope is in him, to the one who seeks him;"
~ Lamentations 3:22-25 (NIV)

10

Your Pulpit Is in the Field

"Keep on loving each other as brothers and sisters. Don't forget to show hospitality to strangers, for some who have done this have entertained angels without realizing it! Remember those in prison, as if you were there yourself. Remember also those being mistreated, as if you felt their pain in your own bodies." ~ Hebrews 13:1-3 (NLT)

God told me very clearly, "Tre, you will do the work of those who refuse to get their hands dirty. Most anyone can reach people inside of a building (the church) but I am sending you to go get my widows, my orphans, and the lost because you understand loss and abandonment, but more than that you understand the power of being found and redeemed." When I was first ordained, I went out expecting that God was going to do things in a way that was powerful and evident. I did not understand that sometimes the greatest power and evidence of who He is comes directly out of brokenness.

By now, I truly understood the authenticity of one's testimony is directly affected by the truth and influenced not by sympathy but instead by empathy. We can reach out and greet someone else's misfortunes, but it takes a different and deeper transparent level of humility to walk in those same tattered shoes.

It is this sentiment that brings life to this bit of wisdom expressed by Theodore Roosevelt, "Nobody cares how much you know, until they know how much you care." God reached me in the darkest of places. It was now up to me, through His guidance, to let others stand up on the floor of my pain so that they would understand that they, too, could have a way not only up, but out.

Newly married, now, I had a different level of praise on my purpose. I was not just thinking about the goodness of the Lord, I could taste the tears of my testimony. Having come through the doorway of despair I could now see the glimmer of hope that shone through the window of God's blessings. I recognized the pain that I had come through when I saw it on the faces of others.

My pulpit happened to be right within the walls of the Horne VA. By the time I made it into 2019 I could not help but tell others about His grace and mercy. There is a special group of ladies that work in an office on the fourth floor that call my "their pastor." Why is this significant? They all attend their own churches and have their own pastors, yet they all know my story and we have built relationship firmly on the foundation of God's Word.

Those ladies have experienced triumph, heartache, heartbreak, and loss within those walls. God has placed me in a position to walk alongside them on their individual journeys. Time spent in their office ministering to them about life and cracking jokes when we are there is a truly unique and special time.

When I open the door on their floor it is not uncommon to walk in and hear, "Hey Pastor," or to be on the phone and have them say, "Pastor needs to talk to you." As I look back on my journey with God's people in that "little congregation," I can truly say that crossing paths with them and being able to have them trust the God in me makes being their "pastor," one of the great honors and joys of my life.

I have many sisters in the faith walking those halls as well. It is not uncommon to hear a strong "Hey, Brother," when they see me in the halls. I will often ask any one of them if they are okay and follow up with something like, "I don't have to come and move furniture, do I?" When they hear that they know I have shown up to check on them. That and a phrase that they say has become one of my signatures, "Hey beautiful people!" And let me not show up for a while, I will hear about it as soon as they see me next. I am just humbled and thankful that through obedience to the Lord I have been able to see miracles manifest in real time.

I have been privileged to have some transformative conversations with some great brothers in the faith that I share the VA campus with daily. Being able to interact with them, to be uplifted, and challenged in the Word of God has brought me strength many a day. There have been more than a few days when they have interceded on my behalf. Focused prayer, especially in a mode of crisis, has a way of making the enemy mad because he gets reminded that he has no dominion in the first place.

Even as a pastor there are still plenty of moments when I must catch myself and refocus. I will get challenged at those times like this, "Excuse me brother, I thought you were supposed to be a man of God?!" In one exchange I remember saying, "All of that is true, but the first word in that statement, 'man of God,' is the word man and as a man, I do not lay down to get run over!" Even in ministering to others I must remember that some people will not recognize the need to defend me, they just expect me to have words of comfort, encouragement, and instruction for them. In return, however, those same ones often forget to return the encouragement themselves.

In spending time with the Lord daily and figuring His course of action for me for the day ahead, I pray this simple prayer,

> "Dear Heavenly Father, thank you for renewing Your mercies for me this day. Show me who to talk to, when to talk to them, and how. If it is not for me to talk directly to someone, give me the strength and courage to look inward and upward, that I may hear from, and be obedient to You. By the authority of Jesus Christ and in His Mighty Name, Amen!"

Being obedient to what I ask of the Lord daily has allowed me to see the great move of God within those walls in the workplace for some time now. I am extremely excited for what He is going to do next.

Many times, just when I think that I am not being effective or that I am not reaching someone, God will send confirmation in a hurry. It is important to note that people are impacted more by what you do than what you say. They appreciate someone who takes the time to listen to them and give thoughtful support.

I really do believe that we have gotten too comfortable being impersonal as a society. When we say, "How are you?" people have been conditioned to hear, "I'm fine," or "I'm okay," and keep moving about their day. But what happens that one time someone says that they are not okay? Do we take time to bless them with a listening ear or dismiss them and their problem as a burdensome part of an already crowded and task filled day?

I choose to try to make peace amid the chaos. As former president Barack Obama says, "Learning to stand in somebody else's shoes, to see through their eyes, that's how peace begins. And it's up to you to make that happen. Empathy is a quality of character that can change the world." It is up to us to turn on the light switch of hope and keep switching it on until the darkness has no choice but to fade.

Isaiah 26:3 (AMP) says, "You will keep in perfect *and* constant peace *the one* whose mind is steadfast [that is, committed and focused on You—in both inclination and character], Because he trusts *and* takes refuge in You [with hope and confident expectation]." Many times, when people are struggling it is important to give them a reason to want to reach out and touch it, that hope! In those times, I try to stand and intercede for them in faith, expecting God to move. But it can be hard for them to see a future in the storm clouds of the present. David Odunaiya says, "Faith and hope work hand in hand, however while hope focuses on the future, faith focuses on the now."

Even though I have a home base out here in the field of the VA Hospital, my wife and I have truly seen God move in the lives of strangers we have met along our journey out and about through divine appointment. It has not been uncommon to be talking to our server at a restaurant and hear a bit of what they are going through only to have those same interactions end with prayer and praise, washed in God's anointing.

I had been doing research on churches in our local area that our family could attend. The Word of Life Faith Center had been great to Stella and me, but it had been a full 40-minute drive from our house so to find a place of worship a little closer to us would be especially important.

We had gone out and visited some churches, but something just felt out of place at each stop. So, I kept looking. I had a very specific set of criteria that I was looking for. Finding a place for our autistic son to be accepted was important, as was access to tools that would allow all of us as a family to be challenged and fed spiritually. The atmosphere had to be authentic too.

How could I be reaching God's people in the field but not be sitting still long enough to be reached myself? We decided that we would give the House of Light Church, located a ten-minute drive, from our house, a try. The first thing that struck Stella and I was that we had arrived early for service and still had to be seated out in the foyer and would watch the service on a television screen in the church's lobby.

Even so, the atmosphere we had been seeking was present and we felt like this was a place we could come back to and worship. We just felt welcome. There would be another service at a location downtown and we would attend that as well. In attending both services we knew that we just had to come back.

That same week they had a class geared specifically toward those in the autism community. These classes met once a month and allowed parents to ask questions and gather resources to help them reach, teach, and empower not only the children, but especially the parents themselves.

As that class wrapped, Stella heard some people talking in the main sanctuary. They were having the new members orientation class. We decided to take a seat and find out a little more about what was going on.

This week helped put our family on a trajectory that would truly allow us to take off and grow together. LightHouse had not only what we were looking for, but especially what we needed. Before I came into the lives and Stella, her mother, and her children they had lost so much. People who were supposed to show up didn't. People who were supposed to stay left. Still others, though tasked with filling them with hope, would leave them empty and unprotected.

It was time for that to change. It was time to start letting them see the best of what could be. It was time to let them not only see but feel and experience what loving them in the right way was supposed to feel like. It was time to see them start winning!

Stella and I now had a full toolbox of equipment that could help us as we set out to reach God's people together. The deep sense of connection that we lost at Word of Life had been replaced with a peace and actions of faith that would be vital to our growth moving forward.

I would need to lean on some of those tools quickly. For most of the last eight months I had been watching my pay checks, expecting that the income withholding order that the judge put in place to garnish child and spousal support from my wages would be executed.

The pay days would come and go without the money being pulled. This really started to weigh on me. I was trying to make sure that I did not give anyone a reason to send me back to prison for failing to fulfill my obligations, especially to my children. I would have a few conversations with Wesley during this time.

During one conversation he would ask, "Do you remember David in Psalm 40?" I did but as is often the case when Wesley is trying to tell me something, I was interested to see where he was going with this, so I stayed quiet. "Remember how David kept waiting on God and when he didn't hear from Him, he just kept waiting? Don't think God is not hearing you. You are in a ditch right now, but God will lift you out. He just wants to hear that you NEED Him," he would say.

As he was talking, I looked up Psalm 40:1-2 (MSG): "I waited and waited and waited for God. At last he looked; finally, he listened. He lifted me out of the ditch, pulled me from deep mud. He stood me up on a solid rock to make sure I wouldn't slip." Wesley would continue, "A year ago you would have been lost trying to figure out why this was happening. And though you are doing that now, wondering what is happening, your eyes are focused upward on His divinity and not down, looking at your despair. You have come a long way. Just hold on."

Wesley's sound advice had gotten my attention. God had sent the answer I was seeking regarding how to make it through this time. I had my marching orders. It was time, again, for me to walk them out. There were also a few challenges that Stella and I were enduring in the house with the kids and Wesley would provide valuable insight to us both.

Wesley is a basketball coach. His girls travel squad was in Horne for a tournament and he let me know that he was in the area. He was going to head to a local laundromat to wash the team's uniforms. "Why don't you just have him come here. I trust you and if he is a friend of yours, he is a friend of mine," Stella would say. I extended the invitation, which Wesley accepted.

The last time I saw Wesley was in 2015 so it was great to see him on this visit. He would come and sit with us for a solid two hours. During this time, he interacted with the kids and listened to the things that were frustrating Stella and I to that point. Knowing me the way that he does he was able to give Stella some of the answers she had been missing to the test. More importantly, through guidance of the Holy Spirit, he would provide me with answers to Stella's test as well. The way he broke it down challenged both of us in a way that was not judgmental, something that Stella really did appreciate.

"It's not so much that you are not doing something right, bro," he would say, "you just have to learn to speak their language." "Stella, there are certain things about Tre that are nonnegotiable and with his extensive background in food service, food is one of them," he would tell her. For a while, I had been struggling with the fact that the kids were extremely picky eaters and food is something that I cannot stand to see wasted.

Wesley would go on to empathize with me about the challenges ahead, especially raising teenage boys. "I know you, so I know that what I am about to tell you is going to hurt, but you may NEVER hear 'thank you,' or 'I appreciate you,' EVER," he said. I was bracing myself and he continued, "It does not matter to the boys that you are now giving them everything they need, what matters to them is that you are not their father..." He was right. It really did hurt to hear it said like that. But Wesley was telling me a truth I needed to touch, and, as always, he was not about to lie to me. While I was proud to be in the kids' lives, they did not yet see a reason why they should be proud that I was in theirs.

As Wesley got ready to leave Stella and I wished him well

and I prayed for all of us as we had just received a blessing from the Lord that was much needed and I wanted to ensure that my friend, my brother, was covered by the blood of Jesus as he continued to walk in obedience to what God was showing to him.

I knew the value of Wesley and I's relationship but now Stella was beginning to find out how much a treasure that was for me. I was simply doing what Mike Norton was talking about when he said, "Never hold resentments for the person who tells you what you need to hear; count them among your truest, most caring, and valuable friends." I had been wondering for a while what I was missing in trying to reach Stella's children and God let me know exactly what that thing was through Wesley.

God is always where we need Him to be, truly omnipresent. Being out on the battlefield for God was beginning to teach me more about the battle and spiritual warfare that was surrounding me. In deciding daily to seek God, I was making a conscious decision to stand for Him despite it all.

I came to realize something else too. Not everyone WANTS a brother or someone to tell them the truth, some just want to do their own thing with no regard to the consequences spiritually or otherwise. Malcolm X said this, "I believe in the brotherhood of all men, but I don't believe in wasting brotherhood on anyone who doesn't want to practice it with me. Brotherhood is a two-way street."

I was doing the right thing but some of what I was beginning to see as a result grated on me too. In some ways I was getting tired. It felt like I was beating my head against the wall with no relief in sight. But God did tell me I was going to be doing the work that no one else wanted to do. Galatians 6:9 (NIV) says: "Let us not become weary in doing good, for at the proper time we will reap a harvest if we do not give up." In all honesty, I was trying to figure out where the harvest was coming from in certain areas. But the key is to not just be obedient, but to stay obedient!

For me, doing this dirty work was not about proving anyone wrong, it was about proving God RIGHT. I knew that what I was dealing with and the situations I was encountering were only tests to see how committed I was to the purpose at hand. It did not matter that some around me did not *yet* believe what was being presented; what mattered was that I stay committed through the point of conviction. I am not interested in playing games with eternity and people's place in it.

> "Commitment separates those who live their dreams from those who live their lives regretting the opportunities they have squandered." ~ Bill Russell

11

The Setback

Mokokoma Mokhonoana reminds us that "A setback often moves us to a road that is even worse but leads to an even better destination." I had been finding my groove back at work now. I was still dealing with the pain associated with recovery, but I was learning to manage it. All my neck and shoulder movements were not as fluid as they used to be, but I had gotten to a place where I could at least function adequately. Thursday May 16th started like most of my workdays do. Yet, leading into the time of our first break I had gotten stiff on my right side and was in some deep pain.

On my break I went to see my primary care provider. I was examined and sent back to work but told if the situation got worse not to come back to my primary care clinic, but instead to go straight to the emergency room. I had felt pain like this post surgery on my right side but for some reason this pain would not leave. I figured that I would be okay if I kept moving around.

We had one more meal to plate up and set for delivery and docking. A few of my co-workers saw the pain that I was in and told me they would switch positions with me if my pain did not let up. Over the next few moments, I would not get the chance to say much of anything.

Just after 3:00 pm as I was plating up sausage on a china plate my neck and right shoulder went completely limp. I lost my grip on the plate and as it hit the floor, I lost all feeling in my neck and right arm. The plate and my arm were not the only things to drop; the next thing to fall was my head. When the sound of the shattering plate was interrupted by my deeply piercing scream two of my co-workers came running, "Tre, shit, you okay man, shit get help!" Someone else managed to help get me to the office and sit me up in a chair.

The pain was so intense I was sweating, profusely. The rapid response team was called to Nutrition and Food Services immediately. Being that the call went out hospital-wide over the public address system our administrative staff, who was on another floor rushed down to see what was going on.

The nurses would ask me what happened. In response, I managed to let them know that I was only six and a half months past my spinal fusion and that I was a type 1 diabetic. They checked my blood sugar. It was 370. They asked if I could feel their hands and fingers prodding different sections of my right arm and shoulder. I could not.

They let me know that I would have to go to the emergency room. One of my co-workers called my wife and told her to get to the hospital because I was going to have to go to the emergency room immediately. I was strapped to a gurney and wheeled upstairs to the ER. Because of the nature of this scare my neurosurgery team was immediately dispatched and would meet me there.

I was scared. My heart was racing. The pain was skyrocketing. It was not night time but the scripture found in Job 30:17 (AMP) was rattling around in my brain, "My bones are pierced [with aching] in the night season, And *the pains* that gnaw me take no rest." People were scrambling trying to figure out what was going on and the best way to help me.

My wife was headed to the hospital, but it would be a while before she would make it there. Overall, I would spend the next six hours in the emergency room. I would be diagnosed with a deep sprain of my neck and right shoulder. They would prescribe some stronger pain medication for me and they would tell me that I could not return to work for the next ten days.

If you think hearing that news was bad, it had nothing on what would happen on the day that I would eventually return to work.

Things would go from bad to worse. I was literally about to be tested in a way that was going to help define and strengthen my character moving forward. Helen Keller was on to something when she spoke about character, saying, "Character cannot be developed in ease and quiet. Only through experience of trial and suffering can the soul be strengthened, ambition inspired, and success achieved." As if I had not been through enough already, more was coming, and it would leave me to question exactly who I was on a professional level.

The day I was supposed to come back to work I gave my paperwork to my supervisor. He said, "Mr. LaVin, I have to ask you to leave my kitchen. You cannot be here. With what has happened to you, you are now considered a medical liability. Until you are cleared by a medical doctor, I cannot and will not allow you to work inside this kitchen. You can go, you're dismissed." I was both shocked and hurt. "What do you mean, I am a medical liability and can't work? This doesn't make any sense," I would say, more pissed than anything else at this point. My supervisor did not blink. He was actually very serious!

That morning my work assignment placed me next to Stella. I would not get to finish, let alone start the shift because of the news my supervisor had given me. Everyone in the kitchen could tell that I was pissed about something, but they were not sure what. In a rapid and hurried tone, I told Stella what was happening. She got about a 30-second overview. I would exit the department, but I did not go home. Instead, I went to our union office on the 4th floor.

I would spend the entire morning in the union office preparing my paperwork to file a grievance against my supervisor and department. Here I was, having gone through recovery after surgery. I fought and went through hell just to be able to be back at work and be able to function within the boundaries of my new normal. Now *this*! It seemed like my supervisor has hell bent on making sure that I did not work instead of doing everything he could to make sure that I could.

I finished my paperwork and found out that I had a legitimate case. When I informed my supervisor of my intent to file the grievance with the union, he told me that was fine. I asked him if

Thank God At Rock Bottom, Jesus Was The Rock That I Hit!

there was a temporary light duty assignment that he could give me that would allow me to work but under a restrictive set of circumstances that did not violate the doctor's order.

"Light duty assignment," my supervisor would say with a laugh, "you can do whatever you feel is necessary but understand I am not required to give you a light duty assignment because your injuries that you had surgery for were military related, not related to this job." He was correct in a way. The surgery that I had came about as a result of trauma my body sustained while in military service.

In the blink of an eye I countered, "The injury itself may not have happened here at work, but the *reaggravation* of those injuries did happen here at this job, in this kitchen, *while* working, in direct performance of my duties and I was not outside of the scope of those duties at the time." The smirk on his face left... *quickly*! "You can think what you want to think but I am still not required to provide you with a light duty assignment," he said.

Rage was taking over me now, but I managed to keep my cool. "Mr. LaVin, what do you know about reasonable accommodations? That may be a step for you to take. In fact, I gave the lady there your contact information and she should be reaching out to you shortly," he said. After hearing this explanation from him, I asked, "Ok, but what does that even mean, reasonable accommodation?" I knew the answer, but I needed to hear what he would say. His answer was right in line with what I already knew.

I would need to request reasonable accommodations because the medical condition I was dealing with was making it difficult to perform the essential duties of my job. The employee is supposed to initiate this type of request but in some cases the employer can make mention of this stipulation, which is what was happening here. According to the Americans with Disabilities Act, "A request for reasonable accommodation is the first step in an informal, interactive process between the employee and the employer."

As mad as I was, I had to realize that this type of accommodation may be the best way for me to not only keep my job but have a job at all at this point. What was clear, though, was that I could NOT come back to work until a doctor cleared me and gave stringent specifications about what I could and could not do.

Over the next week or so human resources would contact me about reasonable accommodations. Because an "accommodation" was being made, the person making the request could not apply for jobs in a higher pay grade. The job being applied for had to be one that represented pay of equal or lesser value. I could still apply for other jobs on my own merit, but they would not fall in line with the rules governing reasonable accommodations.

As much as I loved food service it looked like I would be headed toward a sedentary job, which meant that I would be behind a desk, not having to exert as much physical activity and getting the rest needed for my neck and shoulder to fully heal. Now, after 21 years in the food service business in some capacity or another I had to look reality in the face and understand that my body would no longer cooperate to allow me to do the job that I loved.

What would I be able to do? I had the ministerial background, the counseling chops, and administrative skills to boot. The challenge would be finding a position that would fit what I was now being forced to do. The week prior to human resources contacting me, seven other administrative positions at the Horne VA had closed. All those represented promotions that I could have gotten on my merit. Now I was stuck...

In times like this it is important to remember that we serve a God that shall supply all our needs (see Philippians 4:19). It was not a matter of whether God would provide, my question was "How?" My mind was running in circles. This was unchartered territory for me. I had to recall something that Dr. P used to tell me in this moment, "let thoughts come in but don't stop to think on them; put them on a wave and let them float away."

I was in motion and things were being set in motion but I was anxious, feeling a lot like Elizabeth Gilbert when she said, "Change is all about motion, motion is all about uncertainty and we are deeply uncomfortable with uncertainty." The correct answer is I was uncomfortable. This new normal was completely different from everything I had either known or internalized to that point on a professional level. I had always been secure in my standing professionally, but this new level of uncertainty had me questioning everything within me and the resolve that it would take to sustain me.

Even with all this happening I still needed to go through the worker's compensation process because I was reinjured on the job. One of the union's executive board members gave me the number to an orthopedic surgeon in the area who could help me. That Friday I called and informed the doctor of my situation. I got an appointment set for the next Monday afternoon.

After examination I was set up for orthopedic therapy three times a week. More importantly, though, I would be medically cleared to return to work. These were my restrictions: no lifting anything above the height of the shoulders, no carrying, no pushing or pulling, and no lifting anything over five pounds. Normally, this may not be such a bad thing but in food service, a set of restrictions like that is like a death nail.

There was no news on the job front regarding reasonable accommodations. Even still, I continued to apply for any administrative jobs that were available. Amid all this confusion, once again, the administrative people in my department dropped the ball. For the second time since dealing with the recovery from surgery my paycheck was short, this time the amount was $50.14. Livid is not the right word to describe what I was feeling this time around. I remember going outside and screaming, "Ok God, where are You? I must be missing something. Did this just happen again with my check? I know my hope is in you but what am I NOT seeing?" I was indirectly referencing Psalm 39:7 (NIV) which asks, "But now, Lord, what do I look for? My hope is in you."

I finally returned to work on Monday June 22nd, a full 37 days after I was sent home in the first place. God was working…I took an interview for a secretary position in the radiation therapy department of the hospital and during my first week back, an administrative officer from the Diagnostic and Therapeutic Care Line (DTCL) came into food service looking for me.

One of the supervisors came and got me from the tray line, "Yo, Tre, there is a lady looking for you. She would like to speak to you over there." I headed that direction. She asked, "Hi, Tre, do you remember me?" "Yes, I interviewed with you a few weeks back," I said. In response she stated, "We were all extremely impressed with your interview and we would like to set up a second interview with our acting Section Chief, are you still interested in the position?" "You bet I am," I said smiling but trying to hide my excitement. My interview was set up for the next morning at 10:30 am.

Was this really happening? By now I still had not heard anything about my reasonable accommodation request, so I was humbled because it was obvious that God heard my cry. One of my co-workers approached and said, "Tre there was a lady looking for you, did she find you?" "Yeah, she did, something about a second interview," I responded. Her face turned serious, "Little bro, they do NOT come looking for people like that, normally they just call, you must have really impressed them! All the best with that…"

I showed up for my interview the next morning. I was escorted back to talk to the Chief. Once there, we had a very good conversation. This was not about asking me questions as much as it was just seeing how well I might fit in with the staff in the department. I felt very good about how this had gone. When the interview was complete the Chief let me know that a decision would probably be made by the end of the day but the bulk of the process and how fast it went from there was up to human resources.

There was now some light at the end of this dark, twisted, and frustrating tunnel. Going through the interview process with the staff in the radiation therapy department gave me the jolt of energy that I needed. It felt good to not be treated like I was broken or damaged, but to be "wanted." But this was a process so I would have to wait to see just how much…

> "If you suffer, thank God! It is a sure sign that you are alive." ~ Elbert Hubbard

> "Suffering by nature or chance never seems so painful as suffering inflicted on us by the arbitrary will of another." ~ Arthur Schopenhauer

12

NOT THEIR FIRST CHOICE, JUST GOD'S

In many ways I felt like the ground I was walking on was sinking sand. Yet, the Lord was still carrying me through. A co-worker and I started having random conversations about sports and music. We had a real cool vibe and just clicked. Over some time, I got to share my story with him. In one conversation he mentioned that he and his girl were getting married.

"Oh yeah? Congratulations, that's good! You deserve that! Not that it matters, but I have officiated a couple of weddings before, should be a wonderful time," I remember telling him. He said, "Oh, okay, right, right...that's what's up!" He would go on to tell me when the wedding was, and that Stella and I were invited. Not much else was said on the matter for some weeks but this interaction would come to be vital later, even if he and I did not know it yet.

Bruce and Harleen, as I will call them here (and they *certainly* know why), are some special people. They are different for sure but that is part of their appeal. Bruce is laid back and does not let much bother him. Harleen, though, is a certified firecracker, who only needs one blink to tell you all about yourself. But together they are sweet people. As I would get to know them, they would become like a brother and sister to me.

I was convinced that the shrapnel left from my incarceration would not allow me to grasp certain things. At times, this method of thought would be so strong on me that I would disqualify myself from things, feeling unworthy. For a while, I had a running dialogue with God where I would ask, "I know You cannot be talking to *me* God. Do you not remember what I did? How can You even use me *now*?" In the shadow of one of those moments God shook me with the promise that reminded me not to forget His benefits because He had redeemed me from destruction, and was now satisfying my mouth with good things (see Psalm 103:2-5).

God did not want me to remember what I did in a way that would have me continuing to eat myself up. He wanted me to embrace what He was *doing*! Jesus is the Alpha and the Omega and the beginning and the end (see Revelation 22:13). What that meant for me was if He was first and will be last then He has *everything* in the middle. When we are all stuck in the middle of unpleasant situations sometimes it is hard to see that the things that we go through are meant for us to overcome in order to help someone else begin to walk in their own overflow and blessings.

The next time Bruce and I discussed his wedding they still had not decided on an officiant. They had a few people in mind but had not secured a commitment. I said, "Let me show you something. I don't know if you will need to do this as another option, but I am an ordained minister myself." I went on to show him my credentials. I just let him know that if he and his fiancé were running out of options, I could help them, if needed. "Bro, the way this thing is looking we may need to go with you, we will definitely keep you in mind."

Over the next couple of weeks, Bruce and Harleen's first choice for an officiant backed out. When I heard about that I took things a step further and emailed them my ministerial credentials. Still again, nothing would be said on the matter for a couple more weeks.

Then Bruce pulled me to the side one morning and said, "Bro, you know the second person we had lined up for an officiant? She got sick and is in the hospital." This news took me by surprise because she was one of our community living patients who lived on the hospital campus and I would see her often. The next time I would ask Bruce about that lady he told me that they had received word that she passed away.

Thank God At Rock Bottom, Jesus Was The Rock That I Hit!

At some point Bruce talked to his wife and they decided that I would be their choice to officiate their wedding. When Bruce told me the news, I was excited. "Yours will be the first wedding that I will officiate on this side of incarceration. It is like a new beginning for me in a way," I told him. As excited as I was, I did not want to come about this opportunity the way that I did. Someone had died! It did not seem fair or right that the opportunity came about this way.

Bruce would tell me, "Tre, you know why we chose to go with you? You are a real cool dude, down to earth. You are honest and real. From the moment we met you have been genuine and stayed that way." "That is humbling. I am truly honored," I went on to say. Bruce continued, "You are authentic. More than anything, that is what drew me to you. My girl is on board too. Maybe this is what we all need, to help each other."

It is true what Robert Ingersoll says, "We rise by helping others." But if I was really going to help Bruce and Harleen in the way that was not only requested but intended, I could not take any shortcuts. Upon accepting his proposal, I made sure to let him know, "If I am going to do this, it has to be done right. When you sign me up, when you get Tre LaVin, you get someone who has a responsibility to not only get you *to* the altar, but most importantly *through* the altar." There could be no shortcuts and I knew it.

That same day I would email them the premarital counseling curriculum that I had created and taught from previously. By week's end I would get both on the phone and we would spend a solid hour laying out expectations that we had for one another in this process and getting to know each other even more than we already did.

I really got an opportunity to understand their backstory and them mine. A level of comfort was established. By conversation's end, they knew that I did not play any games with God, which meant that I did not have time to play any games with them and the seriousness of the task at hand.

Over the next few weeks, I continued to communicate with them. They wanted to get Stella a makeover and let her have a form of "girls' night out." This would be Bruce and Harleen's gift to Stella. On the night that Harleen got Stella out of the house I took the time to settle down and write a script for the unity candle ceremony that the happy couple wanted as part of their nuptials. Stella sent me pictures throughout the night of the different phases of her makeover. Harleen managed to do something that night that surprised even me, by taking Stella's beauty up to another level completely. I was told that what I saw that night was just the beginning. "Wait until the big day, just wait," Harleen would say.

When the rehearsal dinner night arrived, it was time to put into full motion this part of God's plan and begin to let the manifestation play out. With my ability to make people laugh and feel at ease many of the nurses in the wedding party were surprised. They were not surprised by the fact that I was a pastor, they knew that. I guess somewhere along the way they expected the jokester to show up and when he did not, one nurse was thrown for a loop...in a good way.

By the time we finished walking through the wedding rehearsal that nurse said, "I always see you laughing and joking with everyone, I had no clue this side even existed! But that is a good thing though, for real." In response I remember saying, "God is not to be played with, so I don't; I take very seriously the task that I have been given and the mandate that comes with it to bring these two together in covenant relationship with Him." I had some other people's attention now and I continued, "Truth be told my work is only beginning once they say 'I do' on Sunday. It is not enough to get them to the altar; I have to get them through the altar as well." Yet, before I could get to Sunday, I had to make it home. This became problematic once I realized that I locked my keys in my car and everyone had already left the venue. Waiting for roadside assistance would cause me to miss the actual rehearsal dinner and make it home almost two full hours after I originally intended.

When their wedding day arrived, I dropped Stella off at Bruce and Harleen's and headed to meet the groom and some of the groomsmen across town, nearer to the venue. The morning went well but as the afternoon came, I started to get nervous. I was not nervous because I was officiating a ceremony, I was nervous because of what this ceremony represented for me and for the bride and groom.

As we got closer to start time, I took a moment to ponder Philippians 4:6-8 (AMP), which reads,

> "Do not be anxious *or* worried about anything, but in everything [every circumstance and situation] by prayer and petition with thanksgiving, continue to make your [specific] requests known to God. And the peace of God [that peace which reassures the heart, that peace] which transcends all understanding, [that peace which] stands guard over your hearts and your minds in Christ Jesus [is yours]. Finally, believers, whatever is true, whatever is honorable *and* worthy of respect, whatever is right *and* confirmed by God's word, whatever is pure *and* wholesome, whatever is lovely *and* brings peace, whatever is admirable *and* of good repute; if there is any excellence, if there is anything worthy of praise, think *continually* on these things [center your mind on them, and implant them in your heart]."

This occasion was one full of honor and was to be admired not only for the bride and groom on this special day but especially because this ceremony would be one where God Himself would be at the center.

Just before the start I would see Stella. Harleen was right. She had outdone herself. Stella and her beauty were striking! It was well worth the wait to see her. Next, I headed to pray with the groomsmen first and then the bridal party. In prayer I would remind those there to support the bride and groom of the special place they held and the responsibility that they now had. Within five minutes we would be ready to begin.

The ceremony was beautiful. To join these two beautiful people in covenant matrimony with God and each other remains one of the more special things that I have been privileged to do in my life. I had sown good seed into good ground with humility and grace that gave honor to the Most High. Little did I know that those seeds would produce opportunities to join two other couples in holy matrimony before year's end.

Before the night ended, I would hear compliments about how well "I" did. "We have never witnessed a wedding ceremony done this way before," one couple would say. Another would add, "The way you made God and relationship with Jesus a priority in this ceremony is to be applauded. It shows the great level of respect that you not only have for Him, but it shows the manner of respect you command on His behalf. This was very well done."

That last compliment made me feel good. It showed that God's anointing was present and that His place of honor was well kept and established. This journey may have begun with Bruce and Harleen needing to have a service done for them. But what they gave me by allowing me to serve them and the Savior was something that I am not sure I could repay them for. They provided me a natural shot at redemption and a chance for me to see just how far I'd come.

13

Transitions and New Starts

I kept plugging along in food service while I waited to see if I was going to be hired by the radiation therapy department. I was not anxious about the possibility at all. Human resources had dragged their feet for a little bit, but it was not like I had not already been used to that. By now I had been going to therapy for my shoulder for a good stretch. I was beginning to get comfortable in this recovery regiment and starting to regain my strength yet again.

Wednesday, July 10th as I was waiting to start my therapy session, I got a call. It was 4:38 pm and it was the VA calling. I had to catch myself. I did and I answered, "God bless, hello." I recognized the voice on the other end of the line as she said, "Mr. LaVin, are you still interested in the secretary position with DTCL?" "Yes ma'am, absolutely," I responded. She continued, "Great because you are their first choice!"

Over the next few minutes, her and I would iron out start date possibilities and report dates, keeping in mind giving the proper courtesy and respect to food service and the necessary two weeks' notice. Because this was a promotion for me, the effective date of such action would be Sunday July 21st, the start of the next pay period. However, my actual report date would be pushed back to Monday August 5th to account for the two-week window of notice. I called Stella immediately and told her the news. She was both happy and relieved for me at the same time.

At 6:04 pm human resources would send out the email confirming my acceptance of the position, thus making everything official! I was relieved myself. God had proven Himself once again. Just when it seemed nothing was going to get done, He reminded me that He never stopped working on my behalf.

I could have easily given up in this process and lost focus, but I did not! The enemy would not get the satisfaction, not from me. Look at 2 Corinthians 4:8-9 (NIV) which says, "We are hard pressed on every side, but not crushed; perplexed, but not in despair; persecuted, but not abandoned; struck down, but not destroyed." When you can find a way to trust God in times of adversity He can, will, and does bring you out.

Pain is never pleasant and often we take too much for granted when things are going great. Going through adversity and coming out on the other side is one of the best ways to grow. Most times true appreciation does not come without adversity.

Willie Jolley says, "Adversity and challenges are life's way of creating strength. Adversity creates challenge, and challenge creates change, and change is absolutely necessary for growth. If there is no change and challenge, there can be no growth and development." Even as I was being promoted and about to move on from food service, I still had one more test to pass before leaving the department. Looking back now I can honestly say that God placed the right people around me in those next three weeks to ensure that I did not blow my top completely.

I did not say anything about my promotion right away, not until a couple of supervisors came and congratulated me. Then as some co-workers overheard, the cat was officially out of the bag. In the days that followed my every move was not only watched but scrutinized heavily.

I was still on the five-pound weightlifting restriction, unable to push and pull the carts carrying my supplies and products for each meal. So, my co-workers and supervisors had to not only get their things but mine as well. This was grating on everybody by this point and no one felt worse about it than me.

Then one morning the powder keg finally blew! I was working on the tray line and as I went to lift something two supervisors came over to me, seconds apart. "Tre, you *know* you can't do that, if you do that again, you will have to leave the line," one said. My face told on me immediately. I said something and as I did two of my co-workers hurried to my side.

"August 5th, brother, August 5th! Don't blow it now, that's what they want you to do," one would say. The other continued, "Listen, whatever you need we will get it. Just say the word. We know what it took you to get here and now other's jealousy is trying to make sure you don't leave and go to the new job." I was hot! By now they both had their hands on my shoulders. "Let us deal with the supervisors, you just stay focused. The baton is already in your hand and you have rounded the curve. I just need you to get across that finish line," one of them said. I took a deep breath and then two more. "Point taken, thank you," I said.

I wanted to cuss those supervisors out and tell them how stupid and petty their behavior was and that I did not need a babysitter. For a solid month and a half now, I had drawn the ire of most of the supervisors and a few co-workers alike and I was frustrated. Being back at work after the last ER visit had become more of a burden than a help. People were glad that I was working but nobody liked all that it took to get me all I needed to do so with the more stringent stipulations in place. For all involved, my time in food service could not come to an end fast enough.

In the meantime, Stella and I were preparing to close on our new home. As time passed it was getting harder to enforce rules without being able to tell the kids the purpose behind them. I would tell them to clean and they would look at me like, "What for? You ain't nobody anyway." Stella would tell them, "You know Mr. Tre loves you, he loves all of us. You can't see it yet, but trust me, you will."

That explanation worked for a while but at some point, fell on deaf ears. I was trying to show them the value of taking care of what they had so that they could appreciate the better thing that was coming. But not being able to tell them, "I'm telling you all this because we are about to move," made it more of a challenge to get the point across.

Stella and I were dealing with this setback over here and that delay over there on a weekly basis when it came to the documentation that was needed to seal the deal. We were supposed to close on July 15th, but that day got moved back by no fault of our own. Once the day got moved, we had to move other things around like the day that our furniture would be delivered.

We had taken leave from work for the week that we were supposed to close but once it changed, we could not submit a different leave request at work because other people were already scheduled off during that time. We were supposed to get our escrow deposit check back at closing too and we had our finances structured around getting that money back on that day. But that did not happen either and it left us scrambling.

A new date of July 23rd was finally set. But as you now know, it could not go smoothly for me, right? That morning while we were pulling out of the driveway to head to the closing, I got a phone call. They needed one more set of documentation. I went to look for it, but I did not have it. Stella and I continued to head toward the office anyway.

We would be on and off the phone with different people over the next three hours. This process had gone on for long enough already and everyone we were talking to at the time could feel our frustration. Finally, we got the go ahead and were able to close on our home. I was excited for Stella to be realizing her dream of home ownership. It had been quite a journey for us getting here.

I could not wait to get back so we could finally tell the kids. After getting everyone to meet us at the new address Stella and I finally were able to see their faces. Seeing the joy that everyone expressed made the wait and not being able to tell the kids for so long worth it.

Not only was I about to transition professionally but we were making this monumental step together as a family. I knew how blessed I was, and I appreciated the special people that I was able to share this journey with. It was a wonderful moment to observe Stella and her children receiving something that they never had before. God was sending a deeper level of confirmation to me and I was really beginning to grasp it.

Back at work, a couple of other small fires had to be put out before my final day in food service. When that day finally came, I was anxious to get the shift over with. I came in and did what needed to be done. Because my shift tour was different from most everyone else at this point, I was able to leave out of the department on that last day with very little fanfare. As I departed, I wished everyone well and gave a simple wave goodbye, letting them know I would see them in the halls around the hospital. As I walked out, that was that.

Monday, August 5th I reported to radiation therapy and got introduced formally to everyone. I felt out of place right away because of how quiet this clinical environment was. Food service was loud, and something was always going on. This was not the case in radiation therapy. While this was not a bad thing, it was the first of many adjustments I would have to make.

After 21 years of unbalanced schedules and working almost all weekends and holidays I now had a Monday-Friday job with set work hours and weekends off. I also was able to wear my own clothes, not having to concern myself with a uniform. The biggest thing though was having my own office and not having my day dictated by hourly physical deadlines. There were administrative deadlines, obviously, but that was completely different. Over time, I would adjust to the slower pace of the day and that would be a great thing, especially for my body.

My first few months on the new job was filled with a lot of training. My new department had not had a secretary for over a year so many of those duties had been spread out and delegated to many different people across the four departments that made up the diagnostic and therapeutic care line.

It did not matter what training was available, I took it. I physically went around the hospital asking questions and networking so that I could build up my list of necessary contacts. Many answers were not readily available, so I had to go find them. That part was okay with me because it allowed me to keep both my mind and body active.

The more I learned, the more comfortable I got. I rediscovered the joy that I had lost over the previous year in food service. I enjoyed being used as a vessel from God to bring hope to our Veterans that came if for various cancer treatments daily. I was able to embrace new challenges and push myself to limits that I did not know I could reach. That is the thing about trying new things. It's not that we cannot do the new thing, we just have to find a manner of comfort in what is naturally unfamiliar. Doing that and embracing things that I was learning helped me to become efficient in my new role quickly.

Often in life, however, as soon as one thing comes together another thing brings a different level of chaos. That chaotic thing came in a unique set of challenges brought forth by three of my stepchildren over the course of about four and a half months. Let me make something clear here: saying that we will be obedient is the easy part; *staying obedient* is the challenge.

The ways I was challenged tested my resolve. It is difficult at times to be the best version of oneself when people tolerate you rather than giving you a fair chance to prove to them the benefit of having you around at all. The spiritual side of me knew the correct answer. I was supposed to stay still and finish what God told me to finish. I was giving my all and everything I had to these children and after a while I wondered if there was even a point. As time drew on, God reminded me, "Son, as bad as this is, you've dealt with worse, stay the course." Once again, I had my marching orders. It did not matter that I felt like I was walking in quicksand.

As I told you, being obedient is the easy part. Staying obedient though, will truly test everything within you. I am not telling you that I don't get mad, angry, or irritated. Those closest to me will tell you that I have done my share of making them mad, angry, and irritated just the same. I have not come anywhere close to doing everything right, but I know the importance of instilling right into those you care about. I certainly know that it does not pay to be disobedient, PERIOD!

This walk has not been easy but every reward that comes as the result of obedience is one that cannot be taken from you. Look at Romans 11:29 which tells us, "For the gifts and the calling of God are irrevocable." This means that when God gives you something that is for you, He does NOT give it back or change His mind about giving it to you in the first place. In blessing me with new life, new family, new jobs, and a renewed calling He was giving me an opportunity to be my absolute best self. It was up to me what I was going to do with it. Your challenge may not be my challenge, but make no mistake, we all have them, and we all deserve to win. Just know that winning sometimes requires that you lose along the way. Enduring some of the things I endured in this season has prepared me for opportunities yet to come.

The thing about living life is there are lessons to be taught, learned, and applied. After that, it comes down to examples and whether someone wants to set one worthy of being followed. In doing so Jackie Robison famously said, "This ain't fun. But you watch me, I'll get it done." We always seem to be looking for something to fit but opportunity could give a damn if it fits, it just wants somebody to want to take it and make it better than it ever was.

14

THE MIND STRUGGLE IS REAL

Mental health is something that is being talked about more as access to different resources become available. There is, however, still a level of stigma that comes with the topic. It is important to note that for some post-traumatic stress disorder (PTSD), anxiety, depression, bipolar disorder, schizophrenia, and the like are not just topics of conversation but unforgiving ways of life for not only those who suffer from these issues but those who care for the people who suffer for them as well.

There is no singular direct cause of mental illness and it is not always attributed to single events or spaces in time. According to the Centers for Disease Control, "a person's mental health can change over time, depending on many factors. When the demands placed on a person exceed their resources and coping abilities, their mental health could be impacted." Quite simply, mental illness can be different things to different people and no two people will react to a situation or set of stimuli the exact same way.

The bigger problem, it seems, is that most that are confronted with symptoms and situations that fall into mental illness categories either do not want to acknowledge those issues and problems or do not know how. There are few things worse than knowing something is wrong and not knowing why or watching someone you care about suffer and not knowing how to help.

Unfortunately, for many Americans, this is an all too real issue that confronts them or those tasked to care for them daily. Over time it can feel like a person is suffering in silence because the weight of these pressures can easily leave one with feelings of hopelessness.

Let me assure you that there is help available and in looking to find the manner of assistance that best fits, there is nothing to be ashamed of. It does not matter if you are the person directly impacted or the person who is the support for that individual. It is not complicated either and it does not have to be. Yet, we make things complicated by not being able or trying to understand.

Often a major hurdle to help and treatment is denial. No one likes to think or hear that they may be "crazy" or "psycho." Those used to be jokes that people would tell and, in some cases, still do. But those words and stigmas are hurtful. If there are legitimate issues the best way to help is to be there. There will be some good days and bad days. One of the best things to do is to come together to learn how to fight the *issues* together and not *each other*!

In this fight those suffering from mental illness need to know that they have people who care about them and that those same people are on the team to help them be the best they can be from moment to moment. Notice I did not say day-to-day. Mental illness is like that irritating gnat, fly, or cricket that lingers around and waits, all the while annoying the heck out of you. It seems to always rear its ugly head when you are not thinking any thing negative or not having a bad day. Yet, a bad moment, or a string of them can turn a good day bad very quickly, sometimes without prior notice and the aftereffects can leave one reeling for days and weeks at a time.

Something else that is pivotal in this process is to educate yourself. The fear of what you do not know can make dealing with this a nightmare before it ever starts. One of the greatest misconceptions is that your loved one can just get what is bothering them out of their mind or flip a switch and just cut it off. It is not that easy. Trust me, if it was, we would all just do that and move right along with our lives!

I asked Dr. P what she would tell a person or a family who was dealing with these issues and coming in for help for the first time. She said, "I would tell them to be as honest as you can. I cannot read your mind. I won't know what's going on unless you tell me. Once you tell me, I can help you." She paused for a moment before continuing, "Be open. Be transparent. Trust the process. It can work and will work if you let it. You came for help. Come get the help you need and use it to begin the process of healing." Lastly, she said, "Tell the truth, no matter how bad you may think it will make you look."

As I was listening to her something very important came to mind. It is important to understand that your truth is not someone else's truth. The way you internalize events directly shapes your version of that truth and that same truth could look completely different in someone else's eyes. It all comes down to perspective. Truth is not something that you can just look at on the surface. It is imperative that you get to the root of the issues. Often, mental illness has a deep and painful root. Pulling that root out is something that you cannot do in one swift motion because it is likely wrapped around a group of other things that it does not want to let go off. The truth has layers. The strength comes as you find the courage to unpack them.

Some that are affected by the issues that come with mental illness may not want to talk about them because it can be painful to relive the experiences that led them to where they are in present day. Still, others will be more than willing to share, as it can be very cathartic and cleansing for them to do so. As a support person if you have a loved one or person that you care about who is willing to talk about the issues that deeply affect them, LISTEN. At times it will be painful to do so. Just know that your listening ear can be a huge help. Listening, however, does not always give proper perspective as it can be hard for the person listening to direct connect to the trauma experience that they are hearing about.

Something that Stella and I experienced speaks directly to this point. Since I have known Stella, I have been incredibly open and honest about the direct mental issues that I wrestle with every day. She understands them to a point. However, hearing about them is completely different from been involved in something as it is happening.

Tuesday December 17, two years to the day that those suicidal thoughts broke me, started as a normal day. The events of two years earlier were nowhere near the front of mind and I was not actively thinking about anything related to that day. But I was acutely aware of what day it was. Midafternoon around 2:30 pm the flashbacks started. Sitting at my desk, I could see everything just as it was when I was sitting in my car on that morning two years prior. The only difference was that I could not see the rain. Everything else, though, was the same.

I went through all the cues and self-talks taught by Dr. P. I took one of the pills that helps flatten my anxiety curve. After about five minutes I was fine. After work Stella and I headed home. As we were, I let her know what happened to me earlier in the day. "Sorry, babe, are you okay?" she asked. I told her I was fine and kept driving.

As I continued to drive, my hands began to shake. I stabilized my grip on the steering wheel and continued with my deep breathing exercises. Stella looked at me. I could see the deep level of concern in her face. "Babe, pull over, you're shaking bad. I'll drive, pull over," she pleaded. At the next highway exit I pulled over and she started to drive.

A greyhound bus that passed very quickly on the left side of me triggered this attack. It was the same type of bus that rushed past me in the rain two years earlier. As Stella started to drive my breathing accelerated. I was struggling to catch my breath. I called my little sister. By the time she answered I was hyperventilating. I managed to say, "Hi sis, I'm struggling right now, I just need you to tell me it's going to be okay." My sister was trying to understand what I was saying. Once she caught on, she immediately started reassuring me.

My head was throbbing. My ears were ringing. I remember screaming, "Not this time, you will NOT win this time Devil." As if the physical attack was not bad enough, I was in the middle of deep spiritual warfare. Ephesians 6:12 (NLT) details just what I was encountering, "For we are not fighting against flesh-and-blood enemies, but against evil rulers and authorities of the unseen world, against mighty powers in this dark world, and against evil spirits in the heavenly places." By now, I had a firm handle on the handgrip above the passenger side door and was slapping the dashboard in front of me.

Once we got off the highway, traffic on the city streets was crawling. Stella was getting frustrated that we were not able to move any faster. My sister kept reassuring both of us. Much like Dr. P, my sister knew by the sound of my voice that something was seriously wrong. Stella had heard about the severity of my anxiety attacks many times before but as she was finding out being next to me in the middle of one was a completely different animal.

Stella and my sister were scared for me but they both kept talking to and reassuring me. After a while both of their voices were cracking. I was still fighting pain physically and in the spirit. I was sweating profusely, and it felt like my windpipe was closing. I was concerned now because I was literally struggling to catch my breath. When we finally arrived at the ER, Stella rushed inside, and my sister stayed on the phone with me.

Some nurses came out and my car door swung open. Stella was trying to get me out. The nurses were telling her to get off me. My sister was screaming back at them, "Don't tell her that! That is her husband and my brother." She would continue giving them pertinent information regarding age, Veteran and war status and my type 1 diabetes diagnosis. I do not remember much that happened after that but I was glad to have people there to help me the best they could, even though they did not fully understand everything going on, as was the case with Stella.

The nurses were asking if my episode was military related. Stella told them that it was. I was struggling to get the oxygen mask off my face long enough to tell the nurses that it wasn't, and this was a result of flashbacks to two years earlier. I know how scary this event was for me. I could not even begin to imagine how scary this was for Stella and my sister. Once I was discharged, we went to the pharmacy and picked up the medication that was prescribed.

If you have a loved one that is struggling with mental health issues, ensure that you make yourself fully aware of the medications that they take daily and how these medications affect them. Learn what their triggers are, those things that bring events back to their memory. Remember the things that help them calm down. Be present for them because in certain situations they may be far from present in the moment that they are experiencing. Love them. Just because something has happened to them does not mean that they are any less of a person. At different times they may not be able to verbalize what is happening to them. There is great value in your ability to pay attention, especially to those things that seem like small details. Those small details may be the thing that helps save a life!

> "The bravest thing I ever did was continuing my life when I wanted to die." ~ Juliette Lewis

The following poem is one that I wrote detailing my own struggles with PTSD, anxiety, and depression. If you are struggling and suffering with mental illness, I pray that you will find comfort in knowing that you are not alone in this fight!

Tre LaVin

Psychogenic Disarrangement

I'm not writing for impressions or to impress / just looking to shine a light on my distress / there are those who think I have nine lives, just a thought / but there's nothing worse than wanting to commit suicide 9 times to finish me off / for those who think this was a game I'd rethink that / because when things came crashing down I would've loved to hit reset / on the console in order to emerge from the depths of this black hole / been trying to get you to understand the mind within me / housed nothing but fragments left from casings of a shattered mentality / fantasies created from necessity / anything to escape the truth of my reality / from the outside in things were perfect or so it seemed / but from the inside out nightmares took the place of dreams / it is hard to function in the land of a broken mental / as the things that happened there are far from coincidental / waking up in the morning not knowing if things in my right mind will out of focus shift / pains of labor birthing actions of consequence / before you take the first step you must count the cost / as failure to do so will result in all things lost / from here on out I need you to take an empathetic point of view / what if the person I described had become you / trying in vain to do everything to explain / but the only thing all can see is constant and enduring pain / as they lash out, all you get is anger or cursed at / as they are standing in a maze full of helplessness / they want to assist not knowing where to start / first trying desperately not to do anything to make it worse / what I'm describing has millions suffering in silence / stretching the boundaries of what we thought was common sense / we need to stop treating this as taboo and prohibited / and while I'm at it let me take chains off of the unspeakable and restricted / as we can no longer afford to be polite about mental illness / we need to know that this is nothing to be ashamed of / after all this thing fails to discriminate as it can affect you or someone you love / we should also note that this in many forms takes / it's been called anxiety, depression, and many things else and can the self-esteem break / frequent stress can affect one's ability to

Thank God At Rock Bottom, Jesus Was The Rock That I Hit!

function / and in life on the daily can cause significant problems / he can break under the weight of constant adjustments / while she can withdraw putting herself in social isolation / it can be hard to ask for help that you may need, but do not recognize / the worst thing you can do is push away and grow to despise / if you or someone you know needs help here is where you can begin / dial 800 273 8255 press one and help your Veteran / or dial 800 950 6264 where you will be linked in to the National Helpline for Mental Illness and they can help you find many paths to treatment

© 2018 Tre LaVin
All Rights Reserved

15

Prospering in Purpose

Love is so subjective that we often reject it when we become the subject of it. On my journey I had to learn to be okay with God loving me despite my many flaws, missteps, and destructive choices. I had to own the fact that I am not perfect and nothing around me will ever be. When overcoming past hurts it is important to know that once we truly repent, God forgets about what we did and keeps loving us just as He always has. His love is one that we cannot fathom. Look at Ephesians 3:17-19 "that Christ may dwell in your hearts through faith; that you, being rooted and grounded in love, may be able to comprehend with all the saints what *is* the width and length and depth and height— to know the love of Christ which passes knowledge; that you may be filled with all the fullness of God."

We as human beings are capable of loving others, but our love comes with conditions. We will cut our love off from someone and take the short-sided view, often forgetting just how patient God was with us while we were in the middle of our mess. His love reaches far beyond anything we could ever imagine and as I found out firsthand His love will reach deep down to rescue you out of the deepest pits of despair. When we say we won't, God proves again and again that He will!

Loving yourself is important because if you cannot do that you cannot be capable of fully loving anyone else. Barbara DeAngelis explains it this way, saying, "If you aren't good at loving yourself, you will have a difficult time loving anyone, since you'll resent the time and energy you give another person that you aren't even giving to yourself." This sentiment does not just have to do with people. It can include your profession and other things as well.

Mark Twain said, "Find a job you enjoy doing, and you will never have to work a day in your life." When you follow those instructions, natural joy will find you. But even better is finding joy in the Lord. That joy is the one that will sustain you. When you can love yourself and what you do, then you are truly able to prosper in your purpose.

Having a deep love and respect for God keeps me in a place of obedience. It was not always like that, but I am glad that it is like that now. Seeing God move in people's lives is something that brings me great joy and gives me great perspective.

One year after meeting my mother-in-law Stella and I went to her hometown to pick up Mom and bring her to her scheduled cancer treatments. I had been there one time previous but this time I was able to meet her dad and most of Stella's family. As we got closer to town, on a phone call with Mom, she asked me if I could bless her house with prayer and say some words of encouragement to my sister-in-law, Stella's younger sister.

God had already spoken to me on this subject, so I had been in preparation to speak to my sister-in-law and encourage her. When we arrived at the house, I was introduced to most of the family. What happened next, however, was a true move of God that was wonderful to experience. I spoke to my sister-in-law and following God's lead I started speaking the Word. As I finished speaking to her then my mother-in- law asked her other relatives if they needed or wanted prayer.

One-by-one they all said yes. So, I prayed for each one of them. God was revealing things to me in the spirit, leaving some to wonder how I knew such things about them, being that we had never met or spoken. As this was happening some of the other relatives were sent for so that they could get prayer as well. All told 11 of us were gathered in a circle in Mom's living room. Generational curses were broken that day! I had expected to be in the house doing what was asked of me for about 10 minutes, but that turned into an hour and 20-minute move of the Spirit!

In that moment I received the tangible evidence that I was right in step with God like I was supposed to be. I was not only walking in purpose; I was prospering in it! God protected me and continues to do so.

If you are lost, I encourage you to connect with the Lord. If you are tired of always coming up with the short end of the stick, talk to the Lord. If your family is splintered, hurting, or broken, seek after the Lord. But when you talk to Him, BE HONEST! He already knows what you need before you even ask (see Matthew 6:8). Honestly brings you closer to humility. Humility, itself, leaves no room to blame others. No matter what your life's journey has been just remember that people love to tag along when you are doing something for them or ascending toward greatness. We all love the perks that come with things that we do not have to work for.

The views and scenery are spectacular from a certain perch and pedestal. When you fall, however, that high pedestal gives way to the splintered, jagged seat of pain. Do not be afraid to touch that pain, there is a valuable lesson to be taught, if you can get out of your own way long enough to learn it. Once you do, you will have the tools to apply it. Once you apply it get better and don't look back. Your greatness is waiting for you to reach out and touch it.

God will be with You every step of the way. I hope that you will always gain the courage to find Him. Good, bad, indifferent, it does not matter. The love He has for us is one that will keep us always. Even, and especially when we fall. There are so many things in my life that I am truly thankful for. But most of all I am thankful that **WHEN I HIT ROCK BOTTOM, JESUS WAS THE ROCK THAT I HIT!**

Thank God At Rock Bottom, Jesus Was The Rock That I Hit!

Prayer for Life Change

Dear Heavenly Father,

    I desire to see the miracle of life change happen in the life of_____. Change their very heart that it may become steadfast and fixed as they learn to trust in You, according to Psalm 112:7. Remove any bitterness that they may be holding on to that is bringing suffering into their life. May they find confidence in You and an everlasting joy to dwell within, a joy that will become their strength, according to Nehemiah 8:10, as You go forward to complete the good work that You will begin in them, by Your Word in Philippians 1:6, may all the mountains in their life be removed, not by might, nor by power, but by Your Spirit, according to Zechariah 4:6. May they come to understand and walk in the truth of Godly repentance, as opposed to the trap of worldly repentance, finding salvation, according to 2 Corinthians 7:10 and may the power of Your Son's sacrifice manifest and reveal who You are and lead to a deep, impactful, and meaningful relationship with You.

By the Authority of Jesus Christ and in His Mighty Name, Amen!

Tre LaVin

Dear Lord,

    Oh, how wonderous is Your Name! It's me and I'm standing in the need of prayer. I need You to wash me and create in me a clean heart, renewing within a right spirit. The enemy is waiting to destroy me, but I will not give in; I put my trust in Your power and will wait on You, instead. You have not always come when I wanted You to, but You always show up right on time! From heaven it shall rain down on me, bringing the anointing to make the difference in my life. From the rising of the sun to the going down of the same I will clap my hands and praise Your Name. I shall not stray, with You I stay, as I look forward to the day that You, Jesus, will welcome me home. You give me strength to know that as an heir, Your blessings are mine. When people ask me about You, I don't hesitate to let them know that Jesus is real! Even in my hardship, I do worship. I have seen so much in this race, almost quit, and lost my place, but for You, Lord, I will finish this race the only way I know how...walking out the steps, ordered by faith! Thanks to You I have learned to let go and as a result, I seek to honor You as Your empty vessel.

Love Always,
Tre

About the Author

Tre LaVin was born in Fort Worth, Texas and raised in Aurora, Colorado. He is a U.S. Army and Operation Iraqi Freedom Veteran. He is a pastor, husband, father, brother, uncle, and son who is proud to be doing the Lord's work out in the field. He lives in Humble, Texas.

Printed in the United States
By Bookmasters